FACING INTERNET TECHNOLOGY AND GAMING ADDICTION

FACING INTERNET TECHNOLOGY AND GAMING ADDICTION

A Gentle Path to Beginning Recovery from Internet and Video Game Addiction

Hilarie Cash, Cosette Rae, and Patrick Carnes

Gentle Path
P R E S S

Gentle Path
P R E S S

Gentle Path Press
PO Box 2112
Carefree, Arizona 85377

www.gentlepath.com

ISBN: 978-1-7320673-3-2

For more information contact Gentle Path Press
at 1-866-575-6853 (toll-free U.S. Only)

Contents

Preface

We (Cosette Rae, MSW, and Hilarie Cash, PhD) are the founders of reSTART Life, PLLC. The organization has been providing residential treatment to both adults and teens who suffer from Internet and screen addiction since 2009. Both of us were therapists in private practice with many years of experience treating this specific behavioral addiction and we decided to team up to provide a higher level of care to youth and adults with problematic digital tech use, as no one else was doing it. People with behavioral addictions so often need a treatment experience where they can be away from their addictive distractions to get on a recovery path. This is as true for those with gaming disorder and other technology problems as it is for those addicted to drugs, alcohol, sex, and gambling.

In time, we were approached by Gentle Path Press, founded by Dr. Patrick Carnes, to create a workbook designed for young adult problematic technology users. We thought this was a good idea since there is enormous overlap in all the addictions, but people using tech unsustainably have additional and unique experiences and struggles. The seven tasks created by Patrick Carnes in his workbook, *Facing the Shadow*, correlate well with our treatment of internet gaming disorder and behavioral addictions, so we were asked to adapt those tasks for people seeking sustainable tech use. We were honored to be asked and the following workbook is the result.

These seven tasks will be a sturdy foundation for your recovery. They include:

- **Task 1:** Break through denial.
- **Task 2:** Understand the nature of addictive illness.
- **Task 3:** Surrender to the process.
- **Task 4:** Limit damage from behavior.
- **Task 5:** Establish sobriety.
- **Task 6:** Ensure physical integrity.
- **Task 7:** Participate in a culture of support.

Decades of research and clinical experience have taught us that breaking recovery down into defined tasks makes it easier to embrace a healthy lifestyle. As individuals perform these tasks, they learn specific ways to manage problems.

This workbook is intended to be used as part of therapy, either in an outpatient or inpatient treatment program. It also works well in conjunction with Twelve Step recovery programs and non-Twelve Step groups like Smart Recovery. See the Appendix for a listing of such support groups. Experience has taught us that a combination of therapy and some sort of recovery community is the key to success.

Throughout the workbook we will be using case studies and examples of situations that involve both males and females. At times, we will use the pronoun *he* to describe someone in a particular situation. Note that often the pronoun *she* or *they/ their* could be substituted. We use this terminology for simplicity's sake, realizing that internet gaming disorder is an equal opportunity condition.

Introduction

If you were born after 1990, you have probably grown up with a great deal of digital technology. When you were young, maybe someone gave you a hand-held gaming device to keep you distracted when you were bored, or your family bought a gaming console that you played alone or with another family member and your friends. You may have discovered that you loved the gaming experience and often sought it out over other things you could or should have done.

Accessing the online cyberworld provides new, exciting, and disturbing things. You probably discovered porn, online gaming, social media, and endless information on any subject that interested you. Your parents may have limited your access to all of this and the time spent there, with more or less success depending on how determined you were to thwart their efforts and how tech-savvy they were. Soon you learned that with a smartphone in hand, you were granted internet access 24/7, anywhere, anytime.

With all this saturation of digital media, it is not surprising that people get hooked so easily. After all, when we are overexposed to anything that overstimulates the pleasure centers of the brain, there is great risk for addiction. Many people don't think about activities as being potentially addictive, but they can be. They can do the same thing to our brains that alcohol and drugs do. That's mind-blowing for some individuals to accept, but it's true. It's the pleasurable activities that we can do for too long that hook us, like gaming or being online for hours at a time, binge-viewing others playing games, engaging in social media, or engaging in other virtual activities.

With the recent classification by the World Health Organization (WHO), we will refer to people who have lost control of their lives due to Internet, screen time, or video gaming as struggling with "gaming disorder." Some people refer to an individual with this condition as "screen dependent," as a "problematic digital user," or as an "addict." If you know that you struggle to control your video game and Internet use and you know that you're losing that struggle, then that's all you need to say. It's a problem and you want some help with it, no matter what you prefer to call it. We choose to use the term "behavioral addiction" throughout this book because it's succinct in capturing what's happening in the brain.

A Growing Problem

There are millions of problematic Internet and video game users in this country alone. And it's a problem that is growing around the world. South Korea and China have designated it their #1 public health problem. Their governments put money and energy into research, treatment, and public education. So, this is a worldwide phenomenon affecting millions of people of all ages, with young adults outnumbering all other age categories. Recent demographic research indicates that rates of Internet gaming disorder worldwide range from 1 to 13 percent of the general population and 13 to 19 percent of the young adult population. Rates of problematic use in the US outstrip rates of problematic use in Europe, while rates of problematic use in Asia outstrip rates of problematic use in the West.

Our experience working with people with internet gaming disorder is that most of them began to recognize they had a serious problem one to three years before getting any meaningful help. Why didn't they go for help earlier? Chances are, it was one of the following reasons. When you think about your own situation, do any of the following statements sound familiar?

- I don't have a screen or gaming problem.
- Nothing will help.
- What I'm doing is normal; just look around.
- Others are overreacting and just don't understand.
- Gaming isn't my problem; it's depression or anxiety or ADHD.
- I don't want to change; I can't change.
- I can stop if I just try harder (as opposed to trying therapy or recovery).
- I will be OK if I just do less. I just don't want to do less right now.
- I will be OK if I just don't get caught.
- I do it to escape my girlfriend/boyfriend, parents, work or _____ (fill in the blank).
- My use is different.
- No one will understand me; no one will be able to help me.
- Nothing is as enjoyable as gaming or _____ (insert technology activity here).
- My parents just don't get it; they don't understand the gaming culture.
- Online is the only place I have friends.

Your internal voice may give you reasons for not doing therapy or twelve step work by telling you:

- Therapy doesn't work.
- Therapy is too slow.
- Twelve Step groups will not work for me.
- Twelve Step groups are a cult.
- I don't believe in God, so Twelve Step groups are not for me.
- I can do this on my own.
- I do not like the therapist, the group, the program, the Twelve Steps, the people there, talking about myself, or _____ (fill in the blank).
- My situation is different.
- No one will understand what I do.

You can deny that you have a problem, but the problem will defeat you in the end unless you do what you need to do to get better. This book is designed to help you do just that.

Journaling and Why We Do It

As you go through this workbook, we encourage you to keep a journal. You may protest, "A journal? You must be kidding. I don't write by hand. My handwriting is terrible. I hate it!" You could type out your thoughts, but if you do, you have to be sure to keep it private. And there is actually some interesting research that says writing by hand is good for your brain. So, we leave it to you, but we encourage you to get outside your comfort zone and at least experiment with a handwritten journal. Use it to record thoughts or notes about the exercises in the book; these will be valuable to you as time goes on. You can also use your journal if you run out of room to write in this workbook. Feel free to record the "overflow" there.

Remember to keep this process simple. Many people find that a cheap spiral-bound notebook works perfectly. Others prefer a leather-bound diary with high-quality paper. Choose whatever works best for you. To keep your journal organized, label your responses with exercise or page numbers from this book. This will make it easier to review and expand on your responses in the future.

Find a secure place to keep your journal. You need to feel safe to be completely honest if you are going to see the benefits of recovery.

In early recovery it will be recommended that you take some time away from your technology, so we recommend writing your journal by hand. Writing by hand in a physical journal may seem strange, but over time you will get more comfortable with it. We recommend this because we want you to discover learning tools that are helpful and not digital. Keep in mind, there are some people who suffer from such severe dysgraphia that handwriting is not an option; for you, we recommend the following safety actions:

1. Before you write, make sure you are using your digital device in a public place.

2. Tell someone what you are doing just before you begin and just after you finish ("bookending" your journaling with someone willing to hold you accountable).

3. Ideally, you can find an accountability partner who gets a report of your computer use from monitoring software that you've been willing to install (like Covenant Eyes, for example). This person could be your therapist or a sponsor who would check to see that you are only writing in your journal.

4. Don't do anything else but write in your journal.

5. Buy an old-fashioned typewriter.

6. Make an audio or video recording of your comments.

Know that anything you write in an email message or post online is public communication. Blogs, Facebook, Twitter, Snapchat, Fortnite, Reddit, and other social media networks are not appropriate ways to share your most private thoughts.

Don't Wait Too Long to Seek Help

In the last 20 years, as the Internet and gaming have expanded throughout the world, more and more people have died because of their addictive behavior with technology. In Korea alone, there is a growing list of gamers who died at their computers. These were young people who did not leave their game to take care of their physical needs for rest, movement, and sustenance. Their bodies gave out. Just after reSTART opened in 2009, we got a call from a distraught stepmother whose stepson had just had his leg amputated because the blood flow to his leg was cut off for too long from sitting still while gaming. Don't let this be your story.

Chapter 1

Who... Me?

It's two in the morning. Jason is full of nervous anticipation of the challenge and fun that awaits. He's not tired, even though he has slept only three hours in the last two days. He already knows he won't get up for school when 6:15 rolls around. He might not sleep at all. It depends on the success of his "mission." His *guild*[1] is camped out where they know a *boss*[2] is going to show up. They hope the boss will drop some rare armor when they defeat it, and if that happens, they have agreed that the armor will become the property of Jason. With the power this armor bestows, he will be able to protect other members as they *level up*.[3] He'll attain serious prestige in this game fairly soon…if all goes as hoped.

School holds no interest for Jason. It's boring. And his social life? What social life? He hasn't found anyone who likes to game as he does, and the games other kids are into are as boring as they are. That is not how he feels about his online friends. Time spent with them is never boring. They have important things to do in the game. They love each other; they would lay down their lives for each other.

There is a girl in the guild that he really likes, too. They've chatted privately quite a bit. She is ten years older and that is fine with him. If he can get some money together, he'll go visit her in California. There is definitely romance between them. Jason is in love; he's sure she is, too. He has asked his parents to send him there for a visit and they have refused. He hates them for their stinginess and lack of understanding. He knows he'll flunk out of school soon and is glad. He would love to see how upset his parents will be, especially his dad. And it will be a relief to get it over with. He's pretty sure his parents won't kick him out of the home; they will be too worried about their little boy. That will leave him free to play

---

1   The group formed by multiple players, like a clan or team, to achieve a shared gaming goal.
2   A powerful enemy in a game that must be fought and overcome for players to advance or earn points in a game.
3   Increase skill and power by getting a character to a higher level. Characters start at level one and increase their level as they kill enemies, learn new skills, etc.

as he likes and not be hassled by his parents beyond the occasional lecture, yelling, and tears that he knows will come, then pass.

Upstairs, Jason's mother awakens and heads toward the bathroom. She pauses by the stairs and listens. She can hear her son talking into his headset, the sound muffled by distance and a closed bedroom door. A wave of despair and depression sweeps over her. What is going to happen to her son? Can her marriage survive the strain? Her husband blames her for being too lenient with the boy; she blames him for being too harsh. He's angry all the time and never misses an opportunity to throw Jason a verbal barb. It must be devastating to Jason's self-esteem. How can they protect their young daughter from the toxic atmosphere that now pervades the house? She has run out of ideas. It feels to her as if she's watching a train wreck that is happening in slow motion and that she is powerless to stop.

Jason's father wakes up, his body missing the warmth of his wife. He knows immediately that she is listening to their son gaming and grows angry. It will be a while before he's able to sleep again, and this makes him angrier. As he lies in the dark waiting for his wife to return, he thinks about the mess they are all in. He can see so plainly that his son is on a path to nowhere, that he will never be successful in the adult world if he doesn't change course. His wife sees it too, but she feels weak as a result of ongoing family conflict and resists taking strong action with the boy. Jason needs to be kicked out of the house if he fails school, which seems inevitable. Tough love they call it. He believes in it, but his wife does not. She wants help for Jason; he wants to give Jason a good swift kick in the pants. He bridles at the notion that he is somehow to blame for the mess Jason's in. It's a father's job to be the disciplinarian and instill values of hard work. It's not his job to be a nurturer. That's for women who are good at it. Compared to his own father, he's a saint. He has never hit the boy, only yelled at him when he needed it. He does not understand why his son seems to hate him so much. He thinks it must be anger over their recent move, done for his career, combined with the negative influences of the Internet world his son now inhabits. His son is addicted, no doubt about it. The one time they tried to remove the computer from Jason's room, he threatened to kill himself. They believed him. He gave a compelling case for change, so they gave back the computer and breathed a sigh of relief when Jason returned to his normal, withdrawn demeanor, happy when gaming, angry at any interference from parents.

Stories like this are played out around the world every day. Jason is 16, but he could be younger or older. When Jason's parents finally contacted us, his addiction was so entrenched that a formal intervention was necessary. They contacted an intervention specialist who was familiar with video game addiction. The interventionist gathered family and friends, figured out what they all wanted to say to Jason, and made a plan for what would happen immediately following the intervention.

The intervention took place, Jason went to Outward Bound (a wilderness program) for three weeks, and when he returned home, he had no Internet access. He attended group, family, and individual therapy and today is finishing high school. At this point, we don't know how his life's story will unfold. We just hope he is learning how to succeed in the real world. If he can do that, then maybe he will be able to play video games in a way that doesn't throw his life out of balance. However, it is possible that, like an alcoholic, he must *abstain* from the games that he most enjoys if he is truly *powerless* over them.

When you read Jason's story, what can you relate to from your own experience? Write down your thoughts in your journal.

Prior to the intervention, Jason was a 16-year old gamer in denial. Denial is a way to avoid the painful feelings that arise when you take an honest look at yourself. Let's say you've been gaming for the last 20 hours and you're too exhausted to get up for class the next day. You skip class, sleep a while longer, and when you do get up, you start back gaming. This allows you to forget about what you just did. And, if someone asks you how you're doing, you sort of believe your own lie when you say you're doing fine. You tell yourself (and others) that you'll be able to catch up with the material you missed, or make up the exam, or that it doesn't matter and you don't care if it does. Whenever reality starts to break through, you make up stories that soothe your discomfort.

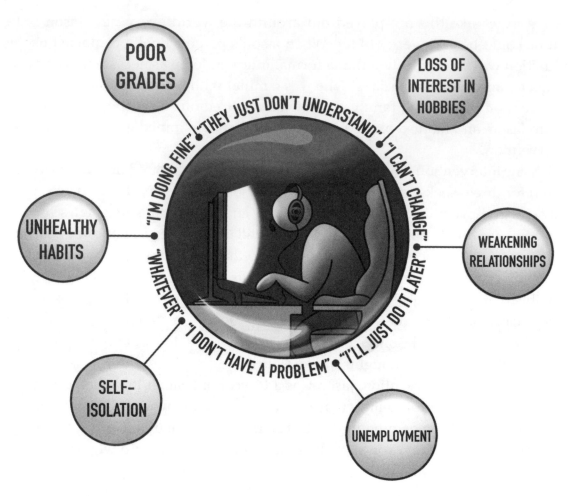

POOR GRADES

LOSS OF INTEREST IN HOBBIES

UNHEALTHY HABITS

WEAKENING RELATIONSHIPS

SELF-ISOLATION

UNEMPLOYMENT

"I'M DOING FINE" "THEY JUST DON'T UNDERSTAND" "I CAN'T CHANGE"

"WHATEVER" "I DON'T HAVE A PROBLEM" "I'LL JUST DO IT LATER"

Figure 1.1

Think of denial as being a thick Plexiglas bubble surrounding you. It distorts all incoming information and perceptions of reality. This, in turn, distorts your thoughts, feelings, and actions. It is only when that bubble of denial cracks and falls apart that you can begin to change.

All in the Family

Who we become as adults has very much to do with the interplay between our biological makeup and the environment into which we are born. How our parents and siblings treat us matters. How much our family has access to financial resources matters. What we observe about the broader culture matters. Our health matters. And so on.

Here, we'll talk about the family itself to explore some of the ways families can influence the development of behavioral addictions. A child's good health, both physical and mental, begins with the feeling of being loved and safe, creating what we call "good attachment." Research is clear on this point. The child who is well attached throughout childhood is at less risk for addictions than the poorly attached child.

Who is going to create that loving, safe attachment? It's the child's primary caregivers who create this (or fail to do so). However, like most things, success to failure falls along a continuum; it's rarely black and white. Sometimes caregivers have difficulty because of their own mental or physical problems. Maybe they are too stressed out or working too hard. Or maybe the parents have their own struggles with substance dependence or problematic tech use. Other parents simply don't know how to constructively support their child.

Different Family Systems

Especially in today's world of widespread digital tech use, parents and caregivers are often spending more time looking at screens than paying attention to their own children. And, more and more, parents are finding screen time for their kids to be very convenient—because a happily distracted child is easy to deal with. So, they give their children screens, not only to keep them distracted, but because they believe there is no harm done and it's making their kids smarter. Add to this the parents who are playing online games with their children, believing this is the way to enjoy time together. Siblings who are watching porn may introduce their younger brother or sister to it. Parents who are watching porn may accidentally leave the screen open for the child to see something that may be both traumatizing and intriguing. Consider the following families:

- A family in which addiction is already present: parents, grandparents, siblings, or extended family members may struggle with alcoholism, compulsive gambling, nicotine addiction, eating disorders, illicit drug abuse, compulsive sex/porn use, or maybe they battle multiple addictions.
- A family where there is a lot of conflict between the parents. This is scary and highly stressful for any child. If there is domestic abuse, it's terrifying.
- A family where there is physical, emotional, or sexual abuse of a child. This is highly traumatizing for any child.
- A family where the parents are cold, critical, and judgmental. This leaves a child always full of self-doubt and self-criticism.
- A family where one or both parents put huge pressure on a child to live up to unrealistic expectations. That child will probably be highly anxious to please or rebel. Or the child will simply give up.

- A family where there have been changes that feel catastrophic to the child, like a divorce, a major move, or a natural disaster.
- A family where the parents are overly involved in the child's life, micro-managing almost everything.

These are all examples of family systems where a child's needs may not be adequately addressed. The unhappy child or teenager is naturally likely to seek escape from the emotional pain of family dysfunction and may turn to something highly distracting and pleasurable like video games, social media, and the Internet. In this way, the groundwork is laid for screen dependence.

Are Digital Devices a New Drug?

Something new is happening in today's world. Sometimes, in the case of Internet gaming disorder, there are no obvious, significant problems present in the family. Instead, loving caregivers who are very consciously trying to be great parents have not realized that when they handed digital devices to their child that they were handing them, essentially, a drug. Because the child was happy and diverted, the child was less demanding and life was easier for everyone. As caregivers looked around and saw that all the families around them were giving digital devices to their children and the schools were promoting the use of computers, they let the child engage with digital technology, not realizing that dependence was developing. *After all*, the parents thought, *This is the new way of the world. All the kids are playing on devices, so why not mine? Besides, this will be making him/her smarter and better prepared for a world dominated by high-tech.* But as time went by, the child may have started fighting with the parents over time spent with devices, particularly when the child's grades started to suffer and the parents began to see a growing problem with the child's tech use.

Whether a child suffers from benign neglect, overt neglect, subtle abuse, overt abuse, or any other circumstance that creates psychological pain, the child must find a way to cope with that pain. This is where gaming and the Internet may be used as a diversion—especially when the parents don't set rules to manage screen time. Even just the pain of growing up can be enough to drive a child to activities that help them escape.

By contrast, in a family that has created and continuously nurtured strong attachment bonds and has found a way to effectively limit and manage online digital use for themselves and their children, the child who is in pain will be directed into other, healthier ways of coping.

With all of this said, we hope you will, by the end of your recovery work, understand the forces that were at work in your own family and why you turned to gaming, screen use, and the Internet as your way to cope.

Exercise: What Was Going on in Your Family That Prompted Your Problematic Internet Use?

_____

_____

_____

_____

_____

_____

_____

_____

_____

_____

_____

_____

_____

_____

_____

_____

_____

Distorting Reality

Internet and video game users have so much experience in distorting reality that they become comfortable doing it. Here are some examples:

- Joe, 19, brilliant, gets into a top tier university but soon fails out. He has been a gamer since he was 12. He loves not only gaming, but watching gaming, reading about the games he loves, and spending time in interesting online fan-fiction forums. Joe believes that these activities make him a part of a special community, one where he feels superior to others who don't share his world. When he lived with his parents, he spent an enormous amount of time finding ways around their efforts to limit his online time. He resented them, believing they were unreasonable. Still, he had enough pressure from his parents that he was able to succeed academically and be admitted to the university of his choice. However, once there, he finds the combination of unstructured time, added social pressure, and untreated depression too much to handle, so he flees into the safety of his online activities. A mild dependence blooms into a more severe one. Joe feels ashamed of his behavior but believes it is impossible to change. He tells no one, believing there is nowhere he can go for help.

- Jared, 26, who has gamed since he was a young child, loses a high-paying, prestigious job as an engineer because his gaming becomes unmanageable. This is precipitated by him feeling intimidated and excluded at work. He is someone who does not know how to speak up for himself very well; instead, he withdraws, feels resentful, and blames others for rejecting him. Jared thinks his boss will not really notice that he shows up late and produces little because he has a great deal of autonomy at his job. Unbeknownst to him, his boss does notice and reaches out to HR.

- Brittany, 20, is a gamer who gets into her top choice university on a scholarship. She has always loved to play massively multiplayer online games (MMOs), but it isn't until she experiences the pressures of university life that her gaming gets out of control. Feeling confident that she can "do it all," she juggles her academic work and gaming while sacrificing sleep. Eventually, her exhaustion catches up with her and she crashes physically and emotionally, shutting down and ending up on academic probation with a 1.5 GPA.

- Aaron, 25, graduated with honors from college and has a good marketing job. He finds himself spending more and more time gaming and looking at porn. He is unkempt and his apartment is a filthy mess. He rarely does anything outside of his job and spending time online. He is one of the top players of his chosen game and he has a following of fans who watch him play on Twitch. Aaron has never dated and has not made any friends since graduating from college. All of his social life plays out online. He thinks this is perfectly OK. He thinks his parents are unreasonably worried about him.

- Tyrel, 17, once wanted to make a career in music. He is also a gamer, a compulsive information junkie, and a viewer of porn. He's struggling with high school because his online activities take up all of his free time. He often does not bother to go to school at all, despite his parents' best efforts to force him to go. The school has not been willing to call a truant officer, so he has no real consequences for his school failure, which he says does not matter to him. He also has stopped practicing piano and writing music. He ignores these consequences and believes that gaming will become a career for him once he is good enough.

- Brady, 22, is a heavy pot user and gamer. He has spent the last four years, ever since failing out of college, living at home, selling and smoking pot and becoming what he believes is a world-class gamer. Brady believes that he will succeed in making gaming his career. The thought of leaving this all behind is intolerable to him because he has invested too much time in gaming to justify giving it up and "wasting all that effort."

- Mario, 25, is suicidal after realizing his "house of cards" is about to come crashing down. He neglected to tell his wife that he lost his job due to gaming. He keeps up the pretense of going to and returning from work, but it is just a sham. He games all day and pays the bills with credit cards. He knows that he cannot continue without his wife finding out.

In each of these cases, there was great difficulty accepting the truth. When these individuals entered recovery, they were stunned by their capacity for self-delusion.

Getting Out of Denial and Into Reality

It is normal for you to feel shame and guilt about your digital behavior. You have not been honest with yourself or others. It's time to be honest with your therapist and support group. The following four exercises will help you work toward getting out of denial and into reality.

The Problem Tree

Directions: This tree is where you will list the problems in your life. These can be problems relating to your use of technology or anything else. Start by writing down today's date in the upper right-hand corner.

Consider the tree trunk your addictive behavior. In the trunk of the tree, write down your primary digital activities. Then, see the branches (with circles) as problems in your life. As you write down those problems in the tree, you may find connections that you hadn't thought about. Maybe your girlfriend or boyfriend just left you or you had a big fight. Maybe the reasons they gave you for leaving didn't include your gaming or Internet use. But, in fact, there might be a connection (and there likely is).

Here's another example of connections you might not have considered. Let's say your car's tires needed replacing. There doesn't seem to be any connection between this problem and your Internet use, but maybe this problem with your car happened because you haven't been earning enough money to get it repaired before it got to the point of being dangerous to drive. Why are you not earning that money? Could it be that you chose screen time instead of going to work?

You see the idea here.

This list will be an important resource as you go through your recovery process. We suggest you plan to discuss with someone (a therapist, your support group, etc.) the feelings that come up when you are doing this exercise. To get the most out of the exercise, you need to make as complete a list as possible. Be aware that this can be upsetting. Prepare to get support as needed.

If you need more space, write down your problems on the lines next to the tree trunk. You can also include more in your journal.

Digging Up Secrets and Lies

Directions: Are you keeping secrets? Are you telling lies? Are you not telling the whole story? Are you saying nothing at all?

All people keep secrets. In the case of screen dependence, it might be how much money users have spent on new games, stealing a parent's credit card to buy equipment and games, meeting up with someone they've met online that they are interested in sexually/romantically, skipping classes, etc.

Secrets themselves are a problem, whether they are outright lies or omissions of the truth. First, you may carry emotional stress from knowing you're being dishonest. You may have anxiety from trying to remember what you said to whom. There is also the fear that someone will discover the truth. You don't feel good about yourself because you may have some strong values about right and wrong but you aren't living by them; in fact, it's quite the opposite. Each of your secrets takes a toll on you. It's time to share your secrets with your therapist and your recovery community. By doing so, those deeply buried secrets lose their power and their hold over you. The result is a sense of freedom and a lessening of shame.

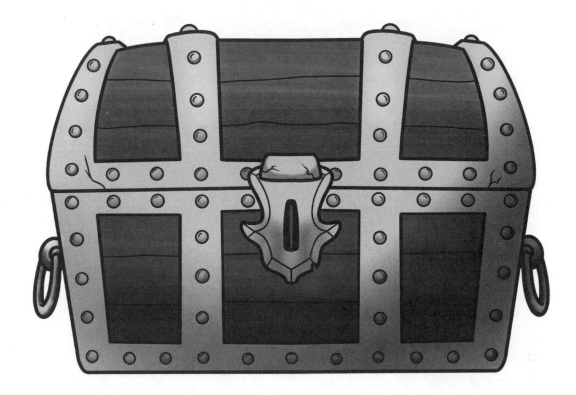

Below, write down your secrets and who you are keeping the secret from.

Secret 1:

_____

From whom have you kept this secret?

_____

Secret 2:

_____

From whom have you kept this secret?

_____

Secret 3:

_____

From whom have you kept this secret?

_____

Secret 4:

_____

From whom have you kept this secret?

_____

Secret 5:

_____

From whom have you kept this secret?

_____

Secret 6:

_____

From whom have you kept this secret?

_____

Secret 7:

_____

From whom have you kept this secret?

_____

Secret 8:

_____

From whom have you kept this secret?

_____

Denial as a Shield

For problematic users of technology, denial is a confused kind of thinking and reasoning. They use denial to avoid the reality of behavior or the consequences of it. Denial is a way to try to manage and explain away the damage caused by addictive behavior. People use denial to protect the behavior that they believe they can't live without. Denial is a way to deflect attention and responsibility, kind of like wearing a shield.

Why You Think You Don't Need Help

Directions: The following are reasons why people feel they don't belong in therapy or a support group for help with their cyber behavior. Circle or highlight the ones you believe to be true, and then write down any additional reasons in the lines below.

- Everyone games and is on their devices all the time, just like me.
- No one was hurt. It's my life, my time, my business.
- My gaming community is where my real friends are; they are the ones who "get me." I couldn't possibly leave them behind.
- I plan to make a living from gaming, so I'm not an addict.
- She games, too, so why is she upset?
- I'll be able to finish my schooling whenever I want.
- This is fun for now and I want to enjoy it while I'm young enough to do so.
- If you think I'm bad, you should see so-and-so.
- My real problem isn't gaming, it's depression (or anxiety, or ADHD, or...)

Additional reasons:

_____

_____

On the shield, make a list of the reasons why you think you don't need or don't belong in therapy, or what kept you from seeking therapy sooner.

Denial Shows Up in Many Different Ways

Directions: The following are different categories of denial. Circle or highlight the examples you can relate to and add more of your own if you'd like.

Deprivation - An attempt to justify your behavior because of some deprivation you suffer.

I feel my life is lonely; I appreciate my online friends.

No one really likes me; people at school are bullies.

I don't have enough money to go out and have fun; I can game at home and it's cheap.

I'm not very social; it's easier online.

I don't do well in school, but I am a pro at gaming.

_____

_____

_____

Global Thinking - Attempting to justify why something is not a problem with terms such as "always," "never," and "no problem whatsoever."

I've never failed a class and I never will.

I can always stop when I want to.

Watching porn is never a problem.

Missing the class test is not a problem because I will be able to make it up.

_____

_____

_____

Rationalization - Justifying your behavior.

> I don't have a problem. I'm just like everyone else.
>
> Older people don't understand us.
>
> I aced high school because I'm smart; I'll be able to do the same in college. My gaming won't interfere.

_____

_____

_____

Minimizing - Trying to make behavior or consequences seem smaller and less important than they are.

> I only game a few hours a night.
>
> It is no big deal; I haven't failed out yet.
>
> I don't need much sleep.
>
> The "F" I got in this class isn't going to matter much to my overall GPA. I'll be able to bring it up.
>
> I don't want a stressful job anyway.

_____

_____

_____

Comparison - Shifting the focus to someone else to justify behaviors.

> I'm not as bad as _____ (fill in the blank).
>
> Compared to my roommate, I don't have a problem.
>
> My little brother spends ten times as much time as I do online.
>
> My parents are on their phones all the time.

_____

_____

_____

Uniqueness - Thinking you are different or special, that some special circumstance or situation causes you to do what you do.

> I am so smart, only the people in my guild can keep up with me.
>
> No one likes me outside of the games because I'm overweight; online, people accept me.
>
> I don't like any of the kids at school; I like my online friends.
>
> I'm the top player on my server; I'm going to be a professional gamer.

_____

_____

_____

Avoiding by Creating an Uproar or Distraction - Being a clown and getting everyone laughing; angry outbursts meant to frighten; threats and posturing; shocking behavior that may be foul-mouthed, sexual, or shocking in some other way.

> I've learned that I can get my parents to back down if I threaten them (yelling, holding a knife, punching the wall).
>
> I've learned that I can get my parents to back down if I threaten to harm myself.
>
> I love trolling and getting others riled up. It makes me feel powerful. It's fun.

_____

_____

_____

Avoiding by Omission - Trying to change the subject, ignore the subject, or manipulate the conversation to avoid talking about what is going on. This form of denial also involves leaving out important bits of information.

Not sharing that you are failing out of your courses.

Not sharing that you didn't show up for classes because of a gaming binge.

Not sharing that you haven't showered in two weeks.

Not sharing that you pee in a bottle so you don't have to leave your computer.

_____

_____

_____

Blaming - Placing the responsibility on someone else.

If my teachers would teach, I'd be happy to go to class.

My parents fight a lot; the only way I can tolerate being at home is to get online.

The girls in my classes are so boring; I'd much rather just look at porn and game.

_____

_____

_____

Hopelessness/Helplessness - Feeling as if all is lost and your situation cannot be improved.

I can't do anything right.

There is nothing I can do to get better.

I'm the worst. Why even try?

Nobody likes me anyway, so I'll go where I can be accepted.

_____

_____

_____

Manipulative and Crazy-Making Behavior - Distorting reality, including the use of power, lies, secrets, or guilt to exploit others. When confronted by others who state a fact, telling them they are totally wrong. Acting indignantly toward them in an attempt to make them feel confused by telling them, in a sense, that they cannot trust their own perceptions.

> I wasn't looking at porn.
>
> You won't have sex with me, so of course I'm going to look at porn.
>
> Here's a (made-up) transcript that proves to you I was attending classes and passing.
>
> I'll kill myself if you take the computer away or kick me out of the house.

_____

_____

_____

Seduction - Using charm, humor, good looks, or helpfulness to cover up insincerity, get others to overlook your behavior, talk others into giving you another chance, etc.

> Come on. That guy just sent me a naked photo without my asking. I wouldn't cheat on you that way. Come here and I'll prove it to you. (This is also crazy-making behavior.)

_____

_____

_____

Denial helps you live with your unhealthy behavior. Right from the start, don't be afraid to label how you rationalize things as excuses for your behavior. Only when you start realizing you're making excuses can you begin stripping away the layer of lies covering your behavior.

Consequences Inventory

People generally expect that others around them will overlook the damage caused by their actions. Some become angry when they *do* experience consequences—being dropped from college, getting kicked out of the house by parents, getting laid off or fired, losing electricity because the bill wasn't paid, and the like.

Consequences, however, are signposts to reality. Individuals experience them because the world does not think how they think. It may take a long time for the consequences to happen, but lies, broken promises, and exploitive behavior will eventually take their toll. As losses continue, many people continue to cling to denial. When that happens, disaster may occur.

For teens who haven't yet graduated from high school, consequences may not be such a big deal. Older teens and adults may find that their consequences are larger and easier to identify.

Directions: Look realistically at the consequences of your behavior in each of the following categories. Circle or highlight any items that describe your experiences.

Emotional Consequences

1. High anxiety, especially around others.
2. Thoughts or feelings about committing suicide.
3. Attempted suicide.
4. Homicidal thoughts or feelings.
5. Feelings of hopelessness and despair.
6. Depression over failed efforts to control your online or video gaming behavior.
7. An uncomfortable feeling like you had two different lives—one in the world and one online.
8. Depression, paranoia, or social avoidance.
9. Loss of touch with reality.

10. Loss of self-esteem.

11. Loss of life goals or failure to develop any.

12. Acting against your own values and beliefs.

13. Strong feelings of guilt and shame.

14. Strong feelings of isolation and loneliness.

15. Strong fears about the future.

16. Emotional exhaustion.

17. Fear of going out of your room.

18. Other emotional consequences: _____

_____

Physical Consequences

1. Continuation of addictive behavior despite the risk to health (e.g., carpal tunnel syndrome, mouse thumb, eye strain, diabetes, selfie elbow, neck pain, sleep deprivation, smartphone thumb, etc.)

2. Significant weight loss or gain due to poor eating habits and lack of exercise.

3. Physical problems, such as ulcers or high blood pressure, deep vein thrombosis, arthritis, etc.

4. Physical injury or abuse by others.

5. Involvement in potentially abusive or dangerous situations.

6. Vehicle accidents (automobile, motorcycle, bicycle) from distracted driving.

7. Injury to yourself from your behavior.

8. Exhaustion from lack of sleep.

9. Poor fitness from lack of physical exercise.

10. Physical consequences related to your sexual behavior, such as erectile dysfunction, sexually transmitted disease, HIV/AIDS, or bleeding.

11. Other physical consequences: _____

_____

Spiritual Consequences

1. Feelings of spiritual emptiness.
2. Feeling that life is meaningless.
3. Feeling disconnected from yourself and the world.
4. Feeling abandoned by God or your Higher Power.
5. Anger at your Higher Power or God.
6. Loss of faith in anything spiritual.
7. Other consequences: _____

_____

Consequences Related to Dating and Family

1. Estrangement from your family of origin.
2. Desiring to date but never dating.
3. Engaging in "hookups" that are without emotional connection.
4. Dating without success at developing a meaningful relationship.
5. Risking the loss of partner or girlfriend/boyfriend.
6. Losing a partner or girlfriend/boyfriend.
7. Increase in relationship problems.
8. Jeopardizing the well-being of your family.
9. Losing your family's or partner's respect.
10. Increasing problems with your children, if you have them.
11. Other consequences: _____

_____

Career and Educational Consequences

1. Failing out of high school or college.
2. Failure to get a job (financially supported by family/friends).
3. Demotion at work.

4. Loss of coworkers' respect.

5. Loss of the opportunity to work in the career of your choice.

6. Falling grades in school; not living up to your academic potential.

7. Loss of educational opportunities.

8. Loss of business opportunities.

9. Forced to change careers or jobs.

10. Not working to your level of capability.

11. Decrease in work productivity.

12. Termination of job.

13. Other career or educational consequences: _____

_____

Some Other Consequences

1. Failure to develop any interests outside of the gaming/Internet world.

2. Failure to develop friendships outside of online communities.

3. Loss of important friendships.

4. Loss of interest in hobbies or activities.

5. You only have friends who participate in or condone your gaming/Internet behavior.

6. Financial problems.

7. Illegal or dark web activities.

8. Lawsuits or any other involvement with the law (including arrests and near arrests).

9. Prison.

10. Stealing or embezzling to support behavior.

11. Other consequences: _____

_____

Talk about what you learned with your therapist or sponsor. This is the tough part. Often this will feel like your consequences are unfair. Remember, there is no promise of justice and fairness in life. In the past, you may have thought others might think you are a good person because of what you have done or how hard you have tried. In reality, it is time to deal with what is happening in your life.

The people or institutions that led to these consequences are not your enemies. When you see those who give the consequences as the enemy, you keep yourself stuck in justifying your behavior. If so, this might help. Think about your consequences as teachers. You have been sent a life lesson. If you don't learn the lesson this time, it will likely manifest itself again—and probably in a more painful way next time. Likewise, unresolved problems may grow worse over time. Learning from mistakes now may reduce harmful consequences in the future.

Accountability Helps You Break Through Denial

In time, most people in recovery discover that taking responsibility for their behavior leads to healthy outcomes. They learn to look honestly at their history and understand how and why their dependence developed as an adaptation to circumstances. This is not easy. But staying in denial and staying dishonest guarantees that old patterns of destructive behavior will continue.

As you begin to accept responsibility for your behaviors and their consequences, you will get a glimmer of what life in recovery can be like. You know how denial creates constant anxiety. Trying to remember which lies you have told to whom is an ongoing source of stress. The good news is that honesty and accountability bring peace and freedom—a feeling of serenity that springs from living with integrity.

In denial, you say that you did not hurt anybody. That's probably not the case. For example, if you act out with compulsive gaming and Internet use, you may want to overlook the ways in which you've used parents or partners for money, or the ways in which you've neglected professional or relationship responsibilities.

In recovery, we talk about powerlessness. You have been unable to stop your behavior on your own. That is why you have reached out for support. Despite being powerless, however, you are still responsible and accountable for what you have done. Being accountable is central to recovery. It will help you break through denial and admit the extent of the problem.

Facing Reality

Directions: Above each of the four figures, write down names of people who have been hurt by your behavior. Inside the figure, describe the ways they have been hurt. Make your examples as specific as possible. *For example, figure 1 is little sister. I hurt her because I stopped paying attention to her.* If you need additional space to write, then continue in your journal.

Before you get started, know that this is one of the hardest tasks in recovery. Though it will be painful, it is not about punishing yourself; rather, it is about facing reality and leaving denial behind.

In Denial, You Are Not Alone

If you are like others, you are starting to realize how far from reality you have been living. To reassure yourself that you are not alone, read the following comments from other technology addicts describing what life was like for them before recovery.

- I often went to sleep at 5 a.m. when I knew my classes began at 8 a.m.

- Missing classes because I was too tired to get up for them became routine.

- Gaming when I needed to be studying for final exams, and then doing poorly in the exams.

- I made a fake transcript to show my parents, to pretend I was attending classes and doing well when, in fact, I spent 3 years of college withdrawing from all classes I signed up for. I was kicked out of college and disowned by my family.

- I was kicked out of college because of academic failure after multiple warnings and offers of help from the university counseling center.

- I lost a full college scholarship because I just gamed instead of doing my academic work.

- I invited someone over that I met in a game (someone I'd never met face-to-face before) and had unprotected sex, even when I didn't want to, because I felt afraid to say "no." This was my first and only sexual experience.

- I never made a single friend at college because I just isolated in my room.

- I used a smartphone app to locate willing sexual partners and took sexual risks with others (unprotected hookups).

- I'd masturbate in my room a lot and rarely study.

- I'm 26 and have never dated. I just masturbate when I want and spend my time online, mostly gaming.

- I lost two close friends because I never returned their calls and never saw them.

- Involvement with total strangers usually began online. Then I would meet them for sex. I even allowed them into my home without knowing them at all.

- Continual texting in my car despite several accidents and near-accidents.

- I stole money from my parents to buy a new gaming computer.

- I accumulated heavy debt to buy valuable in-game items.

- I spent money on upgrading my computer and kept it secret from my partner.

- I left my husband and two children to be with a man I met in Second Life. He turned out to be completely different than I thought he was. It didn't work out, but my husband refused to take me back. Now, I see my kids every other weekend and on Wednesday evenings.
- Whenever I was alone, I felt compelled to game and look at porn.
- I was arrested for looking at underage porn images. I started looking at girls my age when I was 12. I never developed a taste for females who were mature. I spent two years in prison for this illegal behavior.
- I shopped online compulsively and lost all my savings.
- I carried on multiple online relationships. When my girlfriend found out, she asked me to stop but I didn't. Now, I have no girlfriend
- I'm in deep debt because of unsuccessful day-trading.
- I've lost two jobs because I couldn't stop gaming at work, and because I continually showed up late when I couldn't get up on time due to late-night gaming.
- I lost my marriage because I gamed every moment I could, rather than spending time with my wife and being a responsible husband.
- I can't form friendships except in games. I used to have friends, but I now find I'm too uncomfortable with people face-to-face. I'm only comfortable online.
- I had sex with married men I met online.
- I put myself in dangerous situations with strangers I met online.
- At age 14, I already had multiple cybersex lovers that I met in chat rooms. Now I'm 20 and can't seem to ever make a relationship work.
- I've been compulsively looking at porn since I was 8. I sexualize any female I meet, no matter what the age.

All of these people managed to change their lives dramatically. They started by reaching out for support. Are you ready to do that? If so, that's the first step in turning your life around.

Chapter 2
What Does Addictive Behavior Look Like?

When we continually repeat behaviors that we're trying not to repeat, it's called a compulsive behavior. This is the core of becoming dependent, and it relies on neural pathways in the brain. Let's start with a simple explanation. Basically, whenever there is something pleasurable that we can do to excess, it's possible to become addicted to it if we do it too much for too long. This occurs because the brain releases a bouquet of neurochemicals that activate neurons in what is called the *reward or pleasure pathway of the brain.* This produces a "high" or a feeling of relief.

Over time, (it might be short or long), the brain changes to tolerate abnormally high levels of these neurochemicals. We call this *tolerance.* This is the brain's way of trying to return to normal functioning. Being high all the time is not going to work for purposes of survival, so the brain has found a way to adjust in an attempt to function normally. This means the user will no longer get high on what made him or her high before. The user will need more stimulation to get high. If this happens too often, the brain will adjust again and tolerance will increase, depriving the user of the desired high. This goes on until the late stages of an addiction when the individual can no longer achieve either pleasure or relief because the pleasure pathway has adjusted to the point where it has essentially shut down completely. So, why is it so hard for addicts to just stop? This is an important question. The answer is *withdrawal.* Withdrawal is the painful or unpleasant experience addicts go through when they can't get access to whatever they are dependent upon. During the withdrawal period, the body does not have access to normal levels of the neurochemicals that it actually needs for normal functioning. In other words, during withdrawal, the brain is functioning poorly, in a deficit mode. During this period, an internet and technology addict may be depressed or unhappy, angry or irritable, tired or restless, anxious, sleepless, unable to focus, unable to eat, etc.

With substance dependence, withdrawal can also be physical to the point where it is life-threatening. Withdrawal from technology addictions can be equally distressing, though usually not life-threatening. Typically, the individuals we work with report mild-to-severe withdrawal symptoms like irritability, anxiety, agitation, frustration, depression or sadness, nightmares, poor sleep, and *boredom.*

Boredom seems to be one of the strongest and most common experiences reported. This is not surprising, considering Internet users crave the constant stimulation of their screen. When in active addiction, any time they feel the least bit bored, they can pull out their smartphone and surf, game, or check social media. When the over-stimulated mind of a user is deprived of the usual stimulation, boredom is usually the first thing they notice.

The Addiction Cycle

Now that you've learned about addiction from a neuroscience point of view, let's look at it from the point of view of behaviors, thoughts, and feelings. To get started, here are some stories of young people who were caught up in their addiction to online activities.

- Kevin, 22, sought help because he felt close to suicide. In high school, he'd been a gamer, but his strict parents put tremendous pressure on him to succeed academically and limited his personal computer time. He did get into a college. However, once there, he stopped caring about academics and focused solely on gaming. When the university finally dropped him and sent a letter to his parents, the gig was up, his cover was blown, and all hell broke loose. His father disowned him immediately. He lived like a pauper for a few years, living off the money he'd earned in high school, and lived an isolated, shut-in life (what the Japanese would call "hikikomori"). When his money finally ran out, he felt desperate because he couldn't imagine being able to leave the house and go to work. The only world he knew and felt comfortable in was his virtual world. Desperately depressed, he confided his suicidal feelings to his mother, who found treatment for him.

- Carla, 18, was placed on academic probation at college because her casual gaming became a hardcore addiction. She found the increased pressures at college, both social and academic, very anxiety producing. Her way of coping with this anxiety was to escape through gaming. She began to withdraw from friends and family. In just a few months, she spent $10,000 on items for her "free-to-play, pay-to-win" game. This was money intended for her support through the school year. Her parents first realized how badly things were going for her when they noticed the money was gone. They stepped in to help. Thankfully, she knew she was in serious trouble and accepted support.

- Jim, 25, failed out of college because of his addiction to an MMORPG. He married his high school sweetheart and moved to a new city where he got a job in the IT field. He had promised his wife that he would never game again, and he kept that promise for a year. However, eventually, in secret, he found he could not resist the game that had filled his thoughts all during that year of abstinence. He developed elaborate rituals to fool his wife. First, he got up with her and dressed for work. She left first and, as soon as she was out of the door, he rushed to his computer to join the game. He promised himself that he would only play for half an hour, but half an hour regularly turned into half a day. Some days, he was online gaming until just before his wife got home and he quit, left the house, and returned home at the right time to fool her into thinking he was getting home from work. Eventually, of course, his offline world collapsed.

- Kathy, 30, had a similar problem. She was a "romance junkie," addicted to swiping on Tinder. She was married at 24, but had an affair going even on the day of her wedding. During three years of marriage she had never been without one or two lovers, with numerous flirtations on the side. She went to a therapist who told her she was a sex addict. This made her furious because it was so clear to her that she had simply married the wrong man and was now trapped. Then she discovered Tinder. She would pretend to work at her computer until her husband was asleep at night, and then she'd go on Tinder to search for Mr. Right. Although she would set a goal of being in bed by 11 p.m., that seldom happened. Some nights it was 5 a.m. before she dragged herself away. She suffered extreme fatigue. Her ability to perform at work diminished. Professionally, she felt like she was barely treading water. It just kept getting worse. If she could only stay within the limits she set for herself! But she couldn't.

Kevin, Carla, Jim, and Kathy were caught in a repetitive cycle. We call this *the addiction cycle.* This cycle consists of the following four phases:

1. Preoccupation/Anticipation
It starts with being preoccupied with thoughts of doing what you want to do. For example, you might daydream about the upcoming release of some new game or an expansion for your game.

2. Ritualization
Here, you go through habits that have become rituals before going online or once you're online. Example: you go buy soda and chips, set those up by your gaming station, etc. You feel high with anticipation. All other thoughts are tuned out.

3. Compulsive Acting Out
This is when you act on the plans you've made. For example, you spend hours gaming, you start looking for porn or hookups, or you check your phone continually for social media updates.

4. Despair

This is where the acting out is over (for now) and you feel horrible as reality sets in. For example, you've missed final exams. Now what? Are you going to be kicked out of school?

Your Own Addictive Cycle

The following graphic shows the addictive cycle. There is space for you to fill in examples from your own life. Give as many examples as you can.

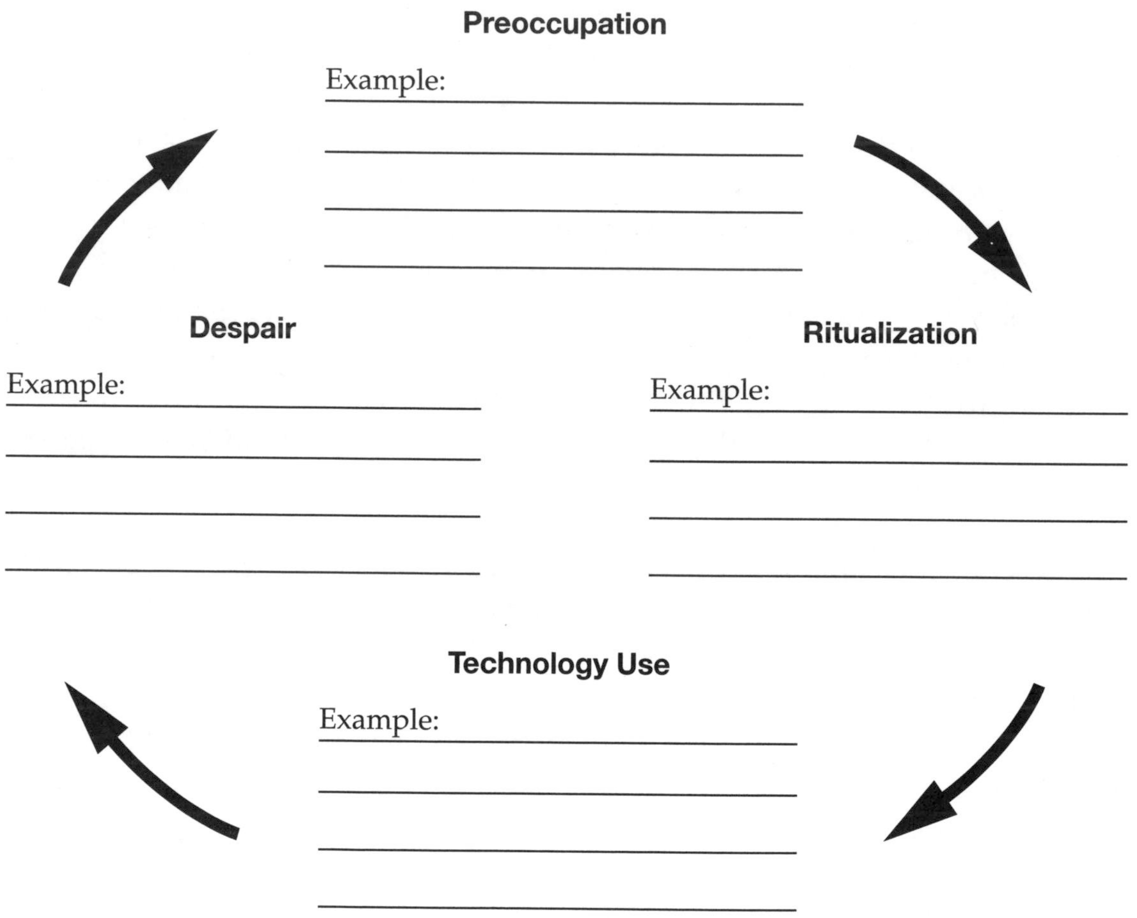

Preoccupation

Example: _____

_____

_____

_____

Despair

Example: _____

_____

_____

_____

Ritualization

Example: _____

_____

_____

_____

Technology Use

Example: _____

_____

_____

_____

Figure 2.1

The Addictive System

The addictive cycle is part of something bigger: the *addictive system.* The addictive system shows how we are all embedded in a family, a peer culture, and the broader society. All of these influence us and impact our addictive behaviors. The system has to do with beliefs, thoughts, the actual addictive cycle, and unmanageability. In this chapter, you will complete exercises to look at the components that go into your own addictive system.

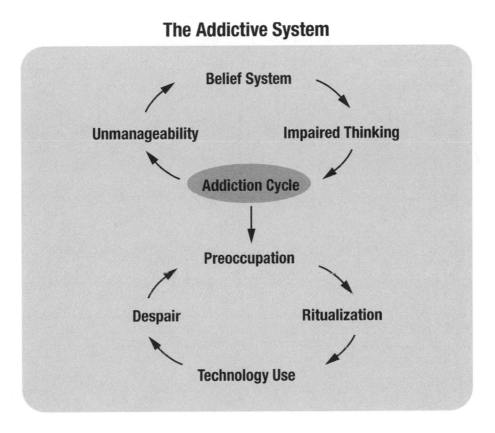

Figure 2.2

Belief System

Here, you will examine the beliefs that underpin your behavior. As you explore your beliefs about yourself and others, keep in mind that all of us have complex personalities, full of contradictory beliefs about ourselves. So, the beliefs you'll tease out here are the beliefs connected to addictive behavior, specifically. You probably have healthier parts of yourself that have healthier beliefs, but the addict self never has healthy beliefs.

People coping with addiction or dependence nearly always have some beliefs in common that go something like this:

1. I'm not worthy of love; I'm a piece of crap.
2. If others actually really knew me, they would reject me.
3. I can't reveal who I really am and what I really need. I'll just rely on myself.
4. I need to get online before anything else. Gaming (or whatever) is my most important need.

Can you relate to these beliefs? Think about times you said these things to yourself. Are there any other beliefs about yourself or others that you are aware of when you really think about this? Journal your thoughts.

Your Beliefs

Directions: What are some of your beliefs? For example, do you ever believe you deserve to be allowed to game while your family supports you? Maybe you believe that you will never be successful outside of gaming. Maybe you believe you've invested so much time in gaming that you need to become a professional gamer to justify your behavior. Maybe you believe that your virtual world and online life is better than the offline world because online you are understood and valued. Maybe you see yourself as a victim offline and successful and valued online. Take your time and write as many beliefs as you can think of.

_____

_____

_____

_____

_____

_____

_____

_____

_____

_____

Addictive Thinking

Although the addictive cycle would never begin without the beliefs in place that we just investigated, there are always thoughts that people have as the cycle begins. These thoughts are tied to feeling the desire to act out (i.e., cravings), and they give us a reason for acting out.

It works like this:

Something triggers your need to go online and do whatever you desire to do. The trigger might be something external (e.g., someone didn't say hi back to you) or it might be internal (e.g., you're feeling exhausted). Whichever way it happens, you're feeling something uncomfortable (anger, fear, sadness, stress, tension, etc.) and you know (often unconsciously) that you can escape your discomfort by getting online right now.

Some part of you knows this is not the wisest choice. For instance, you desperately need sleep, or food, or to study for an exam. But the dependent side of you is able to override these reasonable thoughts by feeding you reasons to go online instead. An example of these thoughts might be: "I'll just game for an hour, then I'll get my studying done." Of course, it doesn't work out this way. Hours later, you're still gaming.

Rationalizing Your Addictive Behavior

Directions: The following is a list of ways you might rationalize your addictive behavior. Place a checkmark next to all of those you can relate to.

_____ No one will know.

_____ Everyone does this.

_____ No one is hurt by my behavior.

_____ It's not real.

_____ It's a good, safe, fun way to escape my problems.

_____ It doesn't affect anyone if they don't find out.

_____ Doing this hasn't changed me in any negative way.

_____ I'm learning good stuff, important stuff.

_____ I feel controlled by others and this is a good way feel free and to get my needs met.

_____ It's a safe way to break the rules.

_____ I can see and explore what I've always wanted to do and learn.

_____ I'm making up for what I've missed.

_____ Those who don't go where I go are just going to be left behind.

_____ This is my world and the way of the future.

Others:

_____

_____

_____

_____

_____

Addictive Cycle

Once you start rationalizing your addictive behavior, the addictive cycle plays out. You become preoccupied, you begin the rituals, you engage addictively, and, when it's over, you probably feel pretty bad.

Unmanageability

The final phase in the whole addictive system is unmanageability. As time goes by, your life begins to unravel. The negative consequences accumulate. Yet, in spite of those negative consequences, you continue these patterns of behavior. This is the very heart of addiction.

Think back to the example of Kevin, who only sought help when he became suicidal. He had been mildly gaming through high school, but this was kept under control by his parents. He wasn't able to game more than two or three hours on any school night (more on the weekends). He got his homework done, had friends that he saw at school, and ran on the cross-country team. He didn't put in his best effort academically, but he did well enough to get into college. He got enough sleep. But when he went off to college where there were no time limits, no bedtimes, no restrictions of any sort, it fell apart. *Freedom! Whoo Hoo! And then, Stress! Boo Hoo!*

It was the perfect storm for his use to rapidly intensify. The combination of academic pressure, social anxiety, unconscious anger at his parents, and freedom to do what he already loved... and over the cliff he went. He was able to hold up in his dorm room and play all day and night. He stopped going to classes, started lying to anyone who asked how he was, felt more and more shame, and became more and more isolated. His life had become unmanageable.

If you're still quite young, in high school, say, the consequences of your use may not be many or severe... yet. But something has gotten you to where you are right now, with this workbook, so there must have been consequences. Maybe they were relatively small compared to other things you're reading about in this book. If that's the case, you're lucky. It would be great for you to get a handle on your problematic behavior early on so you can live a well-balanced life. But to get the benefit from this work, you need to be honest with yourself about the negative effects you are already experiencing. These might be things like conflict at home, not getting enough sleep, a drop in grades, etc.

Unmanageability

Directions: Think of an example of how your own life has become unmanageable. Include when you became aware that you had a problem.

_____

_____

_____

_____

_____

_____

_____

_____

_____

_____

_____

_____

_____

How Do Professionals Know When to Call It an Addiction?

Many professionals *don't* know. Internet and video game addiction is new, first developing in the early 1990s as more and more people got computers, had access to the Internet, and computing improved in various ways.

This addiction is now officially recognized by The World Health Organization (WHO) as Gaming Disorder in the International Classification of Diseases (ICD-11), a manual used by mental health professionals throughout most of the world to diagnose patients. Further research is being done, and the evidence is mounting, showing us that the brain and behavioral changes that we associate with other addictions also occur in gamers and Internet addicts. More importantly, however, it is the pattern of behaviors, common to all addictions, which allow savvy professionals to detect the addiction.

What follows is the list of criteria being proposed for Internet Gaming Disorder in the Diagnostic Statistical Manual of Mental Disorders (DSM-5), the diagnostic manual that is most commonly used in the United States. For the purposes of this workbook, we have changed the wording to account for a broader range of problematic activities related to computers and the Internet. After all, YouTube, Reddit, Tinder, and Google can be just as addictive as gaming.

Do You Meet the Criteria?

Directions: Five of the following criteria must be met within one year to be diagnosed with Internet Gaming Disorder (or Internet Use Disorder). Circle or highlight the ones you can relate to.

- Preoccupation with gaming and/or digital media.
- Withdrawal symptoms when it is not possible to access gaming or the Internet (sadness, anxiety, irritability, boredom).
- Tolerance (the need to spend more time on digital media to satisfy the urge).
- Inability to reduce, or unsuccessful attempts to quit gaming or other Internet activities.
- Giving up other activities or loss of interest in previously enjoyed activities due to gaming and Internet use.
- Continuing digital activities despite problems.
- Deceiving family members or others about the amount of time spent on gaming, etc.
- Using online activities to relieve negative moods, such as guilt, anxiety, or hopelessness.
- Risking, jeopardizing, or losing a job, schooling or relationship due to gaming or other Internet activities.

Write or draw your feelings related to what you've just discovered about yourself.

Collateral Indicators

Directions: Besides looking for the criteria outlined above, a professional will typically look for collateral indicators to confirm their initial diagnosis. These are factors that frequently go along with this addiction. Put a check by each one that you can relate to.

1. _____ I have severe consequences because of my online behavior.

2. _____ I struggle with depression and anxiety.

3. _____ I'm not getting enough sleep.

4. _____ I feel anxious around people and would rather be socially active online.

5. _____ I think I have ADHD; it's hard for me to stay focused.

6. _____ I can see that I use gaming and the Internet to self-medicate (escaping into fantasy to relieve tension, boredom, or loneliness), to soothe myself, and to help myself sleep.

7. _____ I don't date.

8. _____ I don't drive.

9. _____ I don't have much interest in living the life of an adult, with all its responsibilities.

10. _____ I have co-addictions (e.g., weed, alcohol, nicotine, psychedelics).

11. _____ I need to engage with my other addictions to achieve the high I seek when I'm gaming or involved in other online activities.

12. _____ I have a history of deception around my online activities.

13. _____ Other members of my family are addicts.

14. _____ I often feel extreme self-loathing because of my behavior.

15. _____ I have few intimate real-world relationships, sexual, romantic or otherwise.

16. _____ I am in crisis now because of my cyber behavior.

17. _____ I've been in crisis before because of my online behavior.

18. _____ I experience diminished pleasure now from my online behavior.

19. _____ I do not feel close to my family.

20. _____ I do not care much for others.

21. ____ I have not lived up to my potential in school or work.

[reprinted with permission by reSTART]

How are you feeling right now? What are you thinking about?
Now, in your journal or below, write or draw your feelings or thoughts.

Risk Taking and Unmanageability

Directions: Below, you will find a list of other things that are helpful in deciding how severe your problematic Internet use or gaming is. Place a check by each statement that applies to you.

_____ I risked being discovered at home using porn or other unacceptable content.

_____ I was discovered at home.

_____ I risked being discovered at work.

_____ I was discovered at work.

_____ I have experienced diminished or little sleep.

_____ I have engaged in all-night binges with no sleep at all.

_____ I have failed to complete important or scheduled work.

_____ I spent money I could not afford or that was not mine to spend.

_____ I shared personal information with unknown people.

_____ I misused the personal information of others.

_____ I met unknown people for sex.

_____ I was attacked or exploited by internet sexual partners.

_____ I got into entangled relationships that started on the Internet.

_____ My computer was compromised because of viruses or spyware contracted because of online sites or contacts.

_____ I replaced my hard drive or computer because of my online behavior.

_____ I risked arrest because of my online behavior.

_____ I was arrested because of my online behavior.

How are you feeling right now? What are you thinking about?

Now, in your journal or below, write or draw your feelings or thoughts.

How Did I Get to Be This Way?

This is one of the biggest questions asked by individuals in your situation. The answer should become clearer and clearer as you go along in this workbook. For now, we can give you some generalizations based on years of working with young people suffering from Internet/gaming addiction.

- Some users suffer from other mental health problems which have predisposed them to seeking comfort and relief through the Internet. Examples would be having an Autism Spectrum Disorder, Attention Deficit Disorder, acute anxiety, or depression.
- Some users have inherited a genetic predisposition toward addiction.
- Some users were addicted to something else, like gambling or a drug, and switched their addiction to gaming or some other online behavior.
- Some users come from families with parents who are actively misusing drugs, alcohol, or tech.
- Some users come from families where the family relationships did not meet the children's needs adequately.
- Some users come from families where parents were ignorant about the addictive potential of video games and the Internet.
- Some users struggle to create and sustain intimacy. There is a fundamental failure to trust enough to bond with others, and there may well be a lack of relationship skills.
- Some users have a history of childhood abuse, neglect, or abandonment, leading to the mistrust that interferes with intimacy and a desire to escape painful emotions.
- Some users respond to stressful situations such as medical school, business, or danger such as warfare by escaping through addictive behaviors.

Taking a Device Inventory

Directions: Now we'll explore in more depth your online and video gaming behaviors. We'll break them down into categories, but we know that you almost certainly have multiple activities across many categories using multiple devices. You may need to add devices or categories that apply to you that don't appear here. Circle, from the list below, all the devices you currently own (or recently owned). In the next column, write down how many.

Device	How many?
Smartphone	
Dumbphone	
Tablet	
Laptop	
Desktop for work	
Desktop for gaming	
Smartwatch	
VR device	
Augmented Reality Device	
Console device	
Hand-held gaming device	
Implant	
Other	

Now, locate on the house below all digital media devices that were in your home as you were growing up. List them all, along with who owned them and who used them. Also, indicate where they were located in the house, if stationary.

Digital media device	Who owned it	Who used it	Location

Digital Media Activities

Directions: Now it's time to look at what activities you engaged in when you went online. Place a checkmark next to each category that applies to you. This is not a complete list. Feel free to add categories. Be as complete as you can be. Take your time. This is important.

- ❑ Online video games (what genres?)
- ❑ Offline video games (what genres?)
- ❑ Social Networking (what sites?)
- ❑ Surfing
- ❑ Researching
- ❑ Posting/blogging
- ❑ Fan Fiction and other creative writing
- ❑ Seeking and using porn
- ❑ Producing sexually explicit or suggestive content
- ❑ Seeking sexual encounters (online or offline)
- ❑ Seeking romantic encounters (online or offline)
- ❑ Sexting
- ❑ Texting
- ❑ Programming
- ❑ Emailing
- ❑ Shopping
- ❑ Gambling
- ❑ Day-trading
- ❑ Auction sites
- ❑ Other _____

Review what you checked. Think about your behavior in the past and now. For each of the categories of digital media activity, write down the amount of time you spent on that activity, both historically and currently. This exercise will help you realistically assess how much time you've invested in what.

Is There Hope?

Do not lose hope, even if you are continuing to struggle with your addictive behaviors. Recovery is a process, with successes and failures along the way. In the end, we've seen many tech users achieve their recovery goals, but getting there takes time and is not easy. It requires courage to take an honest look at yourself. It takes persistence to learn new ways of being in the world, and new ways of relating to other people as well as yourself. Recovery is no different from learning how to manage any other chronic disease. If you have diabetes, you can learn a new lifestyle to stay healthy. It's the same with an internet gaming disorder. Learning how to live a new, balanced lifestyle is challenging, but worth it!

Chapter 3
Ensure Physical Integrity

There are many physical harms that can develop as a result of too much time in front of a computer screen. The stimulating and mesmerizing effects of the screen and online activities tend to override signals coming from the body regarding the need for sleep, food, movement, and the like. Whether you have been gaming from an early age or did not develop a screen addiction until early adulthood, you can certainly experience negative impacts on your health. It is important and useful to evaluate how your screen time has affected you physically. The exercises in this chapter will help you do so.

Let's start with sleep. Our experience is that most game addicts arrive for treatment severely sleep-deprived. They have not adhered to a regular sleep schedule for a very long time. Instead, they've collapsed into sleep when they simply couldn't stay awake any longer, usually after many, many hours of gaming. The following is a typical story we hear:

> Jake had been gaming since he was 4, starting with Game Boy games. By the time he came for treatment, he was playing a popular RPG for 10 to 20 hours a day, sometimes bingeing for more than 30 hours at a time. He lived in front of his computer, collapsing on the bed only when he couldn't keep his eyes open anymore. Sometimes, 10 to 13 hours later, he would wake up groggy and tired. Other times, he would sleep for only a few hours, then awaken, exhausted but excited to return to the game. The short sleeps were random, without schedule, and never met his sleep needs. The long sleeps didn't begin to make up for all the sleep time lost. It was the excitement of the game, pumping adrenaline into his system, that allowed him to continue in spite of severe sleep deprivation. Had he continued this pattern for much longer, he might have become so sleep-deprived that he would have actually hallucinated while awake, something that we have seen happen.

When a severe level of sleep deprivation is reached, the individual cannot function at full capacity in many areas, cognitively, emotionally, and physically. Common effects of long-term sleep deprivation include:

- Without proper sleep (7 to 10 hours, depending on age) the brain is unable to flush out the toxins that are generated through normal metabolism. There is mounting evidence that without adequate sleep the brain accumulates these toxins, potentially leading to things like Alzheimer's later in life.

- Memories are stored during sleep; therefore, lack of sleep means diminished ability to remember.

- Sleep cleanses, restores, and repairs the body so it can function properly. Healthy weight maintenance depends on good sleep as do emotion regulation and optimal cognitive processes of all sorts. There is, for example, clear evidence that students who are sleep deprived do less well academically, as their ability to pay attention and remember is impaired.

- The lack of a regular sleep schedule, when a gamer ignores their natural biorhythms, can lead to an inability to sleep even when the gamer is trying to sleep. Moreover, the excitement of gaming, combined with the light from screens suppressing melatonin (a hormone that naturally arises in the evening, leading to sleepiness and sleep), may suppress the body's call for sleep.

Sleep Patterns

Think about your recent sleep patterns and gaming patterns. In the space below, describe when you slept, where you slept, and how much you slept over the course of the last year.

_____

_____

_____

_____

_____

Think about how your lack of adequate or regular sleep has impacted you. Write your thoughts below.

_____

_____

_____

_____

_____

Physical Movement

Let's move on to explore how much you physically moved as a gamer and how your lack of movement has impacted you. There is lots of research that proves we need to be physically active in order to be healthy. No matter what your age, being sedentary is the opposite of what you need. Yet, as stated at the beginning of this chapter, the mesmerizing effects of screens can override the body's natural urge to move.

We got a call once from a stepmother, distressed about what happened to her stepson, who was living with his grandmother. He had been sitting for so long in one position while he gamed that it cut off blood from his leg. He was unaware of what was happening—likely because gaming can have an analgesic effect (meaning it numbs pain). The boy's leg was damaged beyond repair and had to be amputated. And, of course, you know the stories of gamers who have died at their computers after playing non-stop for 40+ hours.

These are extreme instances, but, if you are honest with yourself, you will probably be able to identify ways in which your lack of movement while gaming has created some health problems.

Your Lack of Movement

Think about your lifestyle in the past year. How much did you move? Write a bit about that. If you are young and have remained physically active, despite too much gaming, how did your activity levels change because of gaming?

_____

_____

_____

_____

_____

What health effects did this have on you? Did you gain weight? Lose conditioning? What have you noticed?

_____

_____

_____

_____

_____

Diet (Poor Eating Habits)

Now let's turn our attention to diet and the health effects of a poor diet. As you do this, take the time to reflect on how you've been eating while caught up in your addiction. Our experience is that most gamers who need treatment have been eating very poorly. They have been living on fast food and soda, coffee, or other caffeinated, sugary drinks. Their consumption of foods that maintain health is low-to-none: they simply do not eat vegetables, fruits, healthy protein, healthy fats, or whole grains. It is not unusual for gamers, once they start eating well, to lose fat and gain muscle (if they're exercising)—up to 25 pounds in 8 weeks! This happens because they are eating well, exercising, and getting sleep.

Examining Your Eating Habits

In the space below, describe what you ate yesterday. What does a typical day's food intake consist of when you are gaming?

_____

_____

_____

_____

_____

In what ways has your poor diet while gaming impacted your physical health and self-esteem?

_____

_____

_____

_____

_____

_____

Hygiene

Self-care involves the things we have been discussing above, but it also involves things like dental hygiene and showering regularly. Many of the gamers we work with have a poor track record when it comes to their hygiene. The result can be rotting teeth, severe body odor, and acne.

Your Hygiene Inventory

In the space below, write about your hygiene habits when gaming. Think carefully about how often you shower and brush your teeth.

_____

_____

_____

_____

In what ways has poor hygiene impacted your physical health and self-esteem?

_____

_____

_____

_____

Less obvious than problems with sleep, diet, lack of movement, and hygiene are the subtle but critical problems that can arise internally, such as vitamin D deficiency from lack of sunlight, and hypoglycemia (a precursor to diabetes) that arises from too much consumption of low-value/high-calorie foods. It is important that you make an appointment with a doctor to do bloodwork that can identify these kinds of problems. While you're there, have the doctor check your eyes and discuss any other physical ailments you may be experiencing. You're young. There is a good chance you can correct these problems if you catch them early.

Stress and Addiction

If you were to ask gaming addicts whether stress was increased by their internet use, they would scoff and say that internet use was a way to avoid stress, not create it. That myth is dangerous and frequently part of the fabric of denial. Here are the realities about how stress inserts itself into the addictive scenario.

The Hunt. Addiction researchers have documented repeatedly (in many addictions) that part of the addiction is the "search." The anterior cingulate, which is the groove that divides the brain at the top, is the area of the brain used for multi-tasking. It is also built for searching and finding. Mihaly Csikszentmihalyi in his book *Flow: The Psychology of Optimal Experience* describes how the brain always seeks a challenge. He then says that because of this, any obsession rooted in searching can become an addiction. Basically, in addiction the challenge has gone awry.

In trading futures (similar to day-trading), for example, the search for information becomes compulsive and whole days can slip into what we call addict time. The addict does not notice the passing of time. There is real time and then there is addict time. A good example is provided by John, a phenomenally successful 48-year-old trader. The money he made trading futures justified neglecting his children, suffering the loss of three marriages, working 12-hour days, not showing up for family events, and even skipping planned vacations. He was always on the edge of a huge score. The stress of a winning trade was extraordinary. It was also normalizing. After all, who would argue with his success, even though his life was falling apart?

John is hardly alone with his futures trading addiction. Stanford Business School researchers teamed up with brain researchers and found that successful hedge fund managers, when stimulated, showed the same addictive patterns as found in gambling and other forms of addiction.

Online Hunting

Do your online activities involve searching and hunting? If so, can you describe what the ideal "finds" are that you look for? How much of your time goes into the "hunt"?

_____

_____

_____

_____

_____

_____

_____

_____

_____

_____

_____

Risk or Danger

Addiction is also about risk. Trauma research and addiction research are often intertwined. Trauma repetition, as a core part of addictive acting out, recreates in the brain cascades of the stress-related hormones that were present when the original trauma occurred. These hormones are highly addictive neurochemicals we make ourselves. They help us deal with in-the-moment trauma, but, unfortunately, they also take a terrible toll on judgment, brain function, and ultimately physical health.

Bessel van der Kolk uses the phrase, "The body keeps score." This truth manifests in so many ways. Finding dangerous people or situations is one of the hallmarks of this phenomenon. Chris Hedges wrote about how war correspondents would get to the point that they could not have a normal life – preferring to be in a war zone. Studies have shown that many children recreate situations in which they will be abused again, seeking dangerous or illegal activities. Ask yourself: Do your activities online induce risk, danger, or fear?

- Is there preoccupation with traumatic events?
- Do you worry about being discovered?
- Are you obsessed with cleaning your computer for fear of being found out?
- Are you involved with groups that are highly controversial?
- Were you ever involved with groups that were hard to discontinue?
- Are any of your activities illegal or borderline illegal?
- Is there any obsession about specific people out of your personal history?
- Do you have any concerns about anyone finding out about what you are doing online?

Here is one example: Gerald was an older teenager who, through curiosity and an unconscious drive to recreate his own trauma, discovered the Dark Web. There, he witnessed child sexual abuse, murder, and torture. He was retraumatized by what he saw, yet became addicted to it, too.

Living in fear becomes normal at a great cost. Stated simply, the two chemicals that are principle to this process are adrenaline and cortisol. You have probably heard of them, but here is what they do.

Adrenaline mobilizes the body in an emergency so you feel energy, alertness, and strength. Generally, those are desired feelings, and highly addictive. The problem is that you produce adrenaline yourself. So one way to keep the desired feelings coming is to keep your life in turmoil and drama. Unfortunately, if adrenaline is constant, resources of the body are reallocated. If prolonged, the results are:

- The immune system is compromised, and you become more vulnerable to various types of inflammation and infection.
- Your ability to stay focused increases, but over the long term your memory is compromised.
- Your ability to make decisions speeds up, but your capacity to assess danger and consequences can become dramatically less effective.
- Your brain is in overdrive, which reduces your ability to effectively multi-task. Focus trumps keeping track of all that is in front of you.

The companion hormone is cortisol, which is intended to calm things down. This neurochemical regulates sleep, appetite, and cellular function (growth and repair). Thanks to cortisol, the body relaxes and counteracts the effects of inflammation caused by over-stress. When constant, however, the body acclimatizes to its presence, reducing the good things it does:

- Circadian rhythms and sleep are affected.
- Appetite rhythms become problematic.
- Slowing or controlling inflammation ceases to have impact.
- The body's ability to repair and maintain itself is short-circuited.
- The DNA and gene expression become altered and start to impact organ and tissue function.

Please note that the issues raised in this chapter take on new meaning when stress and fear become part of the addictive process. When you know about adrenaline and cortisol, it's easy to understand how appetite, sleep, and weight regulation would be affected.

Risk, Danger, and Fear

Which of your online behaviors make you fearful? Give examples of what you do and how you hide it.

_____

_____

_____

_____

_____

_____

_____

_____

_____

_____

Chaos

Debtors Anonymous (DA) provided both therapists and addicts with a new lens to view stress and addiction. The DA phrase that was used was "fear of the mailbox." It referred to the daily trauma of the debtor getting the mail and all the bad news from people attempting to collect debts, including state and federal agencies. The dread of opening the mail was overwhelming to many.

The insight that blazed a new trail was this: A portion of these people were fully capable of paying, but they procrastinated, constantly failed to add up their own checkbooks, and failed to pay their debts. One client told us, when asked how much money he had, "I do not know. I have not added it up in years." One of the more startling examples in the money disorders is that, in any given group of homeless people, it is not surprising to find people of great wealth. Living in chaos has its own attractions. Among those who have problems with the internet, there is a long list of ways to keep the chaos going:

- Procrastination in many forms.
- Failure to handle finances responsibly.
- Missing deadlines for school or work.
- Overcommitting/underperforming on tasks.
- Making promises and not meeting them.
- Getting involved in "causes" while neglecting their own self-care and maintenance.
- Attraction to people and situations in which high stress is inevitable.

One of the characteristics of addiction is that one loses track of time. So, the logic of being too busy, or having too many "pie plates" in the air, or the demands or "school/work" could be offered to cover for the chaos of your life. The reality, however, may be different. You may use these excuses to paper over your immersion in online behavior while neglecting to take care of the necessary business of your life.

Is Your Life in Chaos

Does your addictive behavior create chaos for you? Provide examples of how you make your own stress. What would you have to do to step away from the many ways in which stress comes into your life?

_____

_____

_____

_____

_____

_____

_____

_____

_____

_____

_____

Living in the Bubble

Digitized media has many examples of people preferring unreality to reality. The whole idea of a "second universe" in which one would rather live has many examples. Even in the early episodes of *Star Trek*, there was the Holodeck where crew members could go and live out their fantasies. The problem was what was called Holodeck addiction, because some crew members did not come back, preferring their fantasies to their responsibilities on the starship. There are countless other examples of people choosing unreality over reality, including pornography, immersion in stories, and the recreation of fantasies in gaming.

People who prefer unreality frequently have significant attachment issues. Relationships with real people bring stress and accountability, as well as the rewards of being part of a larger whole and the comforts of a relationship. Living in the "bubble" of isolation is clinically described as "avoidant," which means the discomfort of loneliness is preferable to having relationships. This, in itself, is a serious problem, as failure to trust others invokes all the stress hormones we have described above.

Even more significant are research findings that have found what is termed "a loss of a sense of agency." What that means is that the person who is living in the bubble will progressively, over time, start to believe that he or she cannot succeed in the real world. They believe they could not compete or hold a job. Nor could they find friends or succeed in love relationships. So, work and intimacy, which are core to mental health, recede on the horizon. In addition, the stronger the bubble is, the more probable severe depression is.

Depression is a very real physical phenomenon that is life-threatening but also treatable. Signs of depression include feelings of despair, hopelessness, and negativity. Sadly, if people believe there is no way they can be successful and this belief continues unchecked, they can reach a state of suicidal thoughts—or action. We have found that the vast majority of clients coming for treatment are depressed and believe they cannot succeed in life. There are some who have reached the point of feeling that suicide is the only way out of their pain.

Do You Live on the Holodeck?

Do you have moments of preferring your life on the internet to what is real? Do you recognize this as avoiding healthy choices for yourself? Give examples of choosing unreality over your real world. Have you experienced despair about this? Can you list examples of hopelessness, feelings of inadequacy, or even the desire to just give up?

_____

_____

_____

_____

_____

_____

_____

_____

_____

_____

Toxic Stress

Most addictions evolve over time and have a common background of toxic stress or chronic traumatic events. Even milder forms of abuse such as child neglect over a long period of time cause changes in the brain. The brain tries to compensate by restructuring itself so the reward systems will compensate for the emptiness and hurt of difficult, hurtful, or harmful events. Many addicts try to normalize their experiences by making excuses or seeing such events as normal and "happening in every family." In treatment and therapy, patients are often startled to realize how they underestimated the impact of what they considered "normal."

Understanding the intertwined relationship between stress and addiction and the impact of stress on your behavior helps you to understand its power. Being stressed may have been an essential component of how your addictive behaviors came to be. Life is really a tapestry of events that record a story that has deep meaning. It is time to ask yourself, has stress always been part of your history, and have you somehow taken it to a whole new level.

Examining Trauma, Threat, Anxiety, and Stress

In your life, have there been extended times of threat and anxiety? Have major traumatic events occurred that have impacted your life? Record what stressors existed in your life before your behavior became problematic.

_____

_____

_____

_____

_____

How connected, in a safe, loving way, did you feel to your family? What connections do you make between your past history and the stress challenges you have now?

_____

_____

_____

_____

_____

Living In Consultation

By now, you realize that working on issues alone is not the way of recovery. We are more effective together than separately. Some of the questions asked in this chapter may seem innocuous and not worth mentioning to others. But others, including your therapist, can help illuminate why these questions and your answers are so significant. Also, some of the questions can be embarrassing or even painful to discuss. Please know that when you want to hide or gloss over something, it is likely extremely significant in your recovery process. Living in consultation means that we no longer hide and everything is on the table for discussion. One of the frequent phrases used in recovery circles is your "best" thinking got you here. It is time to shine light in the dark corners of your mind.

Chapter 4

Problems with Social Intimacy: The Friendship Factor

Sam was just a casual, social gamer. He didn't strive to be particularly good at the game but he loved the social life that he had with all the gamers there. They would spend a huge part of each day talking and joking while others focused on the game. He felt popular and valued. This was the only area of his life where he reported feeling successful. In the offline world, his girlfriend had left him, he was having difficulty at work because he was not showing up very often, and he felt tremendous shame for his situation. In fact, he had become so depressed that he was suicidal. His parents made a surprise visit to him. That's when he confessed his intent to commit suicide. They found a treatment center and he willingly came for help. Today, he is working successfully for a company that offers him a real career path, he is working the 12 Steps, and he is giving back to the world through many recovery avenues. He has good friends and a rich social life. He is now a contented man.

So many of the young people we work with report feeling socially anxious when they have to be around people. It's different when they're online. With a screen and cyberspace between them and whomever they are communicating with, they feel safe and relaxed. They feel free to say whatever they want because they are not face-to-face. They don't really have to worry or care how others are reacting to them. So, the (supposed) anonymity of the communication frees them up to say what they want. If others judge them negatively, they don't necessarily even know it, and they aren't standing next to the person to feel and deal with it. The sense of freedom that comes from this online experience is known as *disinhibition.*

Face-to-face communication is much more complex than any other way of communicating. To be successful at it, we have to learn to decode the many layers of communication coming our way – everything from the actual words said to the tone of voice to the many nuances of body language. It takes practice and is a skill. If you've spent a lot of time in front of a screen rather than out in the world, face-to-face with people, then you may have fallen behind your peers who aren't spending as much screen time as you. You may have the skills of good communication, but you may be "rusty" and lack the confidence to engage with others if you're not online.

During an interview on the topic of Internet addiction, the following story was brought to light. The interviewer described how he had once been a socially skilled journalist, full of confidence around people. Then, he discovered a popular MMORPG and fell quickly into a gaming addiction. He lost his job and everything else he had built for himself as a successful young journalist. Three years later, he was coming out of his addiction (he'd stopped gaming altogether) and was slowly rebuilding his life. What struck us most about this interview was when he told us that he had lost his confidence and his skill around people. Lesson learned: Use it or lose it!

There are also some people who are drawn to the safety of screens because they have a condition that makes it more difficult for them to decode communication. If you are on the Autism spectrum, then you'll need special coaching to help you learn the skills needed to be successful. You will need continual practice in the offline world with other people.

So, why bother? There is a really good reason. It has to do with our need for intimate relationships. You may have friends online that you count as close. You may tell them your secrets, you like them, you value their friendship, and so forth. But there is something you need to know: Those relationships are not an adequate substitute for real-world, face-to-face relationships. The reason for this is *Limbic Resonance*.

Limbic Resonance refers to the release of neurochemicals in the limbic part of the brain that happens when we are in safe, caring, face-to-face relationships with others. We're social beings and we're wired for relationships. We need them in order to be healthy. But it turns out that online relationships don't provide limbic resonance in the same way face-to-face relationships do. Research shows that the more time we spend online, the more depressed and anxious we become. We need to relate in-person for those neurochemicals to be released and to keep us well-regulated both emotionally and physiologically. So, going online to find friends and community is actually the opposite of what we need to do. Yet the allure of feeling safe and relaxed is strong. The allure of finding people who share our interests is strong. The reward of convenience is strong. The fun of anonymity is strong.

Here are a few examples of ways that people have found community online. For some of them, their in-game or online personas feel like their *identity.* They've invested so much time building their reputations and identities that the thought of giving them up is difficult.

- Chuck was quite renowned in a video game. In-game, he had achieved a high rank and was much admired within his game community for his skill and the role he played as a member of his guild. He was a healer and the guild could not advance without him. He considered his guildmates his best friends and swore he would lay down his life for them. They were scattered around the world, so he couldn't do that, but, in-game, his noble sentiment could be realized if the occasion arose.

- Sarah belonged to a writer's forum. She had made quite a reputation for herself, with people from around the world commenting on what she created. She knew they were paying attention to her, whether or not they liked her writing.

- Christopher was a political blogger and was followed by a growing number of admirers (and detractors).

In the following exercise, write about your own online social experiences.

Online Social Experiences

Directions: Think about times in your life that you've avoided face-to-face socializing. When do you remember wanting to avoid people? Do you remember why? What did you say to yourself? What did you do instead? You can write your responses below or you can draw them in your journal.

_____

_____

_____

_____

_____

Do you remember times you were bored and lonely and went online rather than making plans to get together with someone you knew? Describe this.

_____

_____

_____

_____

_____

_____

Do you remember a time when someone you liked wanted to spend time with you and you turned them down? Think about why you did that. What were you feeling and thinking? What did you do instead?

_____

_____

_____

_____

_____

Who is your closest friend? Is this person an online friend or an offline friend? Describe them and what your relationship with them is like.

_____

_____

_____

_____

_____

_____

The Internet and Antisocial Behavior

It's no surprise to any of us that online communities can be antisocial. Social media sites like Facebook, Twitter, and Instagram, along with gaming sites, have become places for bullying, flaming, trolling, etc. In-game conversations are often yelling matches full of swearing, put-downs of all sorts (including the "n-word," the "b-word," homophobic words, and so forth). All of this disrespectful, antisocial communication wires the brain for disrespectful, antisocial behavior. We have seen in our work, especially with teens, a profound lack of respect for one another and the staff, and we have witnessed how difficult it is for these individuals to form friendships because they don't know how to be kind, empathetic, and sociable. Scholars have discovered that empathy has been dropping significantly over the last few decades. It is hard to care and feel compassion for others if you lack the capacity to empathize with them.

Eric is a good example of this. He is a young man of 17 who spent a great deal of time trolling on the Internet. He was a gamer and enjoyed saying obnoxious things to the other gamers and watching their reaction. It made him feel powerful. As a result, he started going into online forums of all sorts and saying things that would upset anyone who was present. This trolling activity began when he was 12 and went on for five years before he was sent to treatment for his Internet misuse. Eric had very few friends offline; in treatment, his highest goal was to make friends, but his actions toward others made this extremely difficult.

What he was used to doing was getting satisfaction by upsetting people and watching their reaction. He continued this behavior in treatment because it was a hard habit to break. It was how he interacted with the world. But interacting in the real world, face-to-face, was different. For the first time, Eric recognized that his trolling behavior caused people to dislike him, and he wanted to stop it. Thankfully, because he was persistent and determined, he slowly broke his trolling habit and began making friends. But let's think about who Eric was becoming and what sort of a man he would have been if he had just continued on his trolling path. Can you relate to Eric's situation?

The following exercise will help you look at your own situation.

Exploring Your Antisocial Beliefs and Behaviors

Directions: List the words that you commonly used when you were online, feeling anonymous and free to say whatever you wanted without consequences.

1. Racial slurs that you've used:

_____

_____

_____

_____

2. What do you actually believe about races that are different from your own?

_____

_____

_____

_____

3. How did you feel when using these slurs?

_____

_____

_____

_____

4. Slurs about sexual and gender identity that you've used:

_____

_____

_____

_____

5. How did you feel when using these slurs?

_____

_____

_____

_____

6. What do you actually believe about people whose sexuality and gender identity do not conform to the norms you were raised with?

_____

_____

_____

_____

7. Slurs about women/girls that you've used:

_____

_____

_____

_____

8. How did you feel when using these slurs?

_____

_____

_____

_____

9. What do you actually believe about women and girls?

_____

_____

_____

_____

10. Slurs about men that you've used:

_____

_____

_____

_____

11. How did it make you feel when using slurs about men and boys?

_____

_____

_____

_____

12. What do you actually believe about men/boys?

_____

_____

_____

_____

13. Other slurs you have used:

_____

_____

_____

_____

14. How did you feel when using these slurs?

_____

_____

_____

_____

15. What do you actually believe?

_____

_____

_____

_____

Now that you've looked at your antisocial behavior and beliefs, are you surprised by what you wrote down?

Think about those beliefs and who you want to be in the world. You may believe that you are superior to some other groups of people. If this is true, there is still the question of how appropriate it is to behave badly around those you feel superior to. Is it OK to be disrespectful?

Think of it this way: If others think they are superior to you, is it be OK for them to be disrespectful to you?

Take some time to reflect on these questions. Write down your thoughts here or in your journal.

_____

_____

_____

_____

_____

_____

_____

_____

_____

_____

_____

_____

In the next chapter, we'll look at dating, sex, and romance. Antisocial beliefs and behaviors can impact who you are attracted to, and who is attracted to you. Antisocial beliefs and behaviors can limit and even hurt relationships, especially when the person you are with does not agree with what you are saying or doing.

Chapter 5

Problems with Sexual and Romantic Intimacy

Now it's time to talk about finding sex and love. The online world, as we all well know, is full of opportunities to explore our wildest sexual fantasies, curiosities, and romantic dreams. It's a world without boundaries, without moral compass, with limitless variety. It's a world that feels like it provides safety because of its supposed anonymity. It's a world where we can be sexually and romantically stimulated without ever having to encounter a real person. It's a convenient world, requiring little effort to find sexual and romantic content to satisfy our curiosity and hunger. Here are a few examples of people searching for sex and love:

- Eva had profiles on Match.com and OKCupid. She had fun (and frustration) with the men who contacted her. What she loved was chatting with them through the website, never actually meeting. She didn't give out her number or location because she preferred the ease of online chatting to the more complex process of phone calls and face-to-face encounters. She felt emotionally safe this way. If someone didn't seem to like her, she felt insulated from that rejection. It was all just so casual, after all.

- Michael was someone who first looked at porn when he was 8. He was revolted and fascinated. He spent a lot of time online in a variety of activities, and the porn was always a part of the picture. At age 22, he had a sexual template that was created by 14 years of viewing porn. He liked the idea of having a girlfriend who would also be a sexual partner but did not have any idea of how to go about finding such a partner. In his first attempt, when he became infatuated with a young woman he met while climbing (an activity he had enjoyed while in a recovery program), he found himself so "love obsessed" that he could not handle her disinterest in dating him. In fact, her rejection sent him into a severe relapse.

- Ben was 12 when he began an online romantic relationship with an adult man, Greg. Ben pretended to be an adult female and it worked. Greg did not ever figure this out. This continued for ten years. In fact, Greg had never seen Ben. They did not Skype; they only texted. As far as Greg knew, Ben was a woman. At age 22 and feeling deeply in love with Greg, Ben was considering having a sex-change operation to become the woman that Greg thought he was.

Online relationships may not satisfy your deepest need for human love and connection, but it can provide the illusion that it does. When someone avoids forming face-to-face relationships, we call them *Socially Anorexic.* When someone avoids face-to-face sexual and romantic relationships, we call them *Sexually Anorexic.*

Many of the young adults we work with are sexually anorexic. Typically, they have a history of either never dating, just hooking up, or, if they've had romantic partners, it hasn't gone well or lasted long. What they have done is use a lot of online pornography. Some have become so obsessed with the porn that they use porn even more than gaming. However, most of the gamers we work with do not invest that much time in porn. Instead, they primarily invest their time in gaming and other online passions, using porn two to ten times a week for masturbation, then getting back to their primary interest.

Let's take a moment to look at the difference between healthy and unhealthy child development in the realm of sexuality and romance.

Healthy Child Development

The course of child development in the Western world for the last hundred years or so has been some variation on what follows: Boys and girls, around age 7, typically separate and play with their own gender (we recognize that things may be different for gay and transgender kids), learning different skill sets. Girls typically learn intimate social/relational skills while boys learn more about team playing/hunting/competing. Once hormones kick in, these kids are drawn to each other and have to figure out how to relate. They first learn how to be friendly, then they learn how to flirt, hang out in groups, and eventually to date. The end goal is to enter into sexual relationships that might be casual or more committed. This adolescent development takes place over several years, usually from around 12 to 18, by which time couples have formed and some of the young adults are getting married.

Of course, there has always been wide variation in this pattern, with some kids becoming sexual earlier or later, some forming couples much earlier or later (or not at all), etc. The main point here is that kids had to learn how to relate to whomever they were attracted, and this took practice—with plenty of mistakes along the way. But those mistakes helped them learn and improve their skills until, at last, they began to be successful.

Unhealthy Child Development

Many of today's young people do not experience this path. Take the case of a teen who has been inundated with porn from an early age. That teen may feel attraction for someone else but, not having much social skill, be afraid to try to connect. It's so much easier to just go home and masturbate to porn and play games. By avoiding social contact, that teen does not learn and practice the skills that would make dating successful. And the longer this goes on, the more entrenched that teen will be in using porn and avoiding the challenges of courtship. Soon, the years go by. The teen is now an adult in his or her twenties and deeply discouraged about the possibilities of successfully forming a meaningful relationship. This is likely to be a person who feels quite a bit of social anxiety whenever an opportunity arises for developing a relationship with someone attractive. The idea of dating a real person who doesn't look or act like a porn star may be a problem, too.

Today's World

Directions: Here are some of the sexual patterns we have seen among the gamers and Internet users that we have worked with over the years. Following each explanation, you will have an opportunity to explain how you relate to each pattern.

Most common. This is the Internet user who masturbates to porn about once a day to relieve his/her sexual drive but is not obsessed with it. The main interest is in gaming and other online activities. This person has zero to little dating experience.

How do you relate to this?

_____

_____

_____

_____

Sexual sublimation into games. This is the gamer who does not feel a strong sex drive. He/she is obsessed with gaming. This individual may masturbate to porn occasionally, but that is all, and will say that he/she has little interest in sex.

How do you relate to this?

_____

_____

_____

_____

Hookups and other imitations of porn. This is the gamer that looks for hookups and participates when the opportunity presents itself. He/she may or may not wish for a long-term relationship, but that is not what is actively pursued. This person is a sexual opportunist and may or may not use hookup apps to assist the search for sex.

How do you relate to this?

_____

_____

_____

_____

Sex and porn addiction. This is the young person who is obsessed with sex to the point of damaging some aspects of life. This obsession may be acted out with others or may remain confined to masturbating to porn.

How do you relate to this?

_____

_____

_____

_____

Manga and anime porn and romance literature. This is popular among gamers, who often prefer reading manga and watching anime porn.

Is this something you like and seek out? What do you go for?

_____

_____

_____

_____

Fetishes. This involves becoming aroused by sexualized objects. A subcategory of this is furry culture, in which both cartoon and non-cartoon porn involves the blending of human and animal forms (e.g., a person is portrayed with fox or cat features.)

For example, the My Little Pony figures were incorporated into pornographic cartoons and became popular among children and teens.

What has been your experience with finding yourself aroused by objects? How did this begin? How strong is that urge?

_____

_____

_____

_____

Long-term committed cybersexual relationships. These are long-term relationships when you rarely or never meet your partner.

How do you relate to this?

_____

_____

_____

_____

Long-term committed real-life relationships combining romance and sex.

How do you relate to this? Is Porn part of your relationship? If so, how? How do you think your partner feels about it?

_____

_____

Is there a category of sexual experience that we've left out but that you've experienced? Please write about it here:

_____

_____

_____

_____

_____

_____

_____

_____

_____

_____

_____

_____

Internet Porn Use

Part I

Directions: Take a moment to reflect on your use of porn. Compare the time you spend looking for porn with your time invested in other online interests.

Estimate, realistically, the hours per week you were involved in some form of online sexual behavior:

Times per week _____ Hours per session _____ Weekly total _____

Now estimate the amount of time per week spent in other online activities:

Times per week _____ Hours per session _____ Weekly total _____

Where have you spent the majority of your time? _____

What's the second priority? _____

What's the third priority? _____

Now reflect on time spent on sites dedicated to romance, flirtation, or other forms of sexual/romantic titillation, such as dating sites or chat rooms, including texting/sexting.

Times per week _____ Hours per session _____ Weekly total _____

Reflection: Now that you have quantified the amount of time you used to spend with porn and romantic distractions, what thoughts come to mind and how are you feeling about this? If you need more space than what is provided, feel free to write in your journal.

_____

_____

_____

_____

Part II

There is a variety of reasons that people give for why they avoid sexual and romantic encounters. The following are some examples:

- Benjamin avoids asking a woman out because he can't handle the anxiety he feels. He's afraid of rejection every step of the way. She may turn him down right off the bat. She may not want a second date. She may not find him good enough as a lover. If she really got to know him, she would surely not love him because, deep down, he's really a piece of crap.

- For Bobby, the challenges of learning how to date just feel insurmountable. Too much work. He feels he's fallen too far behind to ever catch up and learn how to be successful.

- George finds that real women just aren't attractive to him. They don't look like the porn stars he watches and fantasizes about. He'd rather stick with fantasy than reality.

- Scott discovered one time when he was hooking up with someone that he had ED (erectile dysfunction). He was mortified and never wants to experience that again. He was only 19 at the time.

- Samantha is overweight and afraid she will be rejected by any man she hopes to date.

- Butch likes the ease, the convenience, and the tidiness of masturbation. No having to deal with another person's bodily fluids or their emotions. Too complicated. Too messy.

- Terry loves the flirtation game. She feels totally free in her online communications to be as sexual and raunchy as she wants. An in-person dating situation, however, makes her very nervous. She would rather skip all that, avoid entanglements, and just enjoy the fun of online flirting.

- Steven, who first discovered BDSM porn as a 13-year-old boy, is afraid that any person he dates will reject him because of his fetish. He knows that he could find a BDSM partner through websites, but he is afraid of the actual encounters. The fantasy will do.

- Mark is confused about his sexuality. He's watched every kind of porn out there and finds himself turned on by it all. Is he gay? Is he straight? Trans? Pansexual? He has no idea. He doesn't want to date, in large part, because he doesn't know who he is.

Have you ever avoided in-person dating and intimate relationships, instead choosing porn or some other online sexual/romantic activity? yes   no

If so, what were your reasons?

1. _____

2. _____

3. _____

4. _____

If you identify with being a sexual anorexic, let's look at some of the *beliefs* about yourself that may be in play. These are beliefs that keep you stuck in your social and sexual anorexia. Here are some examples that might capture some of your own beliefs. There is space to add beliefs that apply to you but aren't listed.

- No one would want me.
- I'm too shy to date.
- I'm too weird to date.
- I can't handle the pressure of dating.
- I'm OK just with porn and online friends.
- _____
- _____
- _____
- _____

Most problematic users have an *intimacy disorder.* Their ability to relate well to others, to develop deep, trusting relationships that satisfy their deepest needs for love and sex requires personal development through committed recovery. It takes work and it's worth it.

It's time to explore whether your behavior meets the criteria for sex addiction. If it does, you will need to work on this along with your Internet gaming problems. Just answering six questions in the test below will help you look honestly at your sexual behavior and help you make some decisions.

PATHOS

Directions: The PATHOS is a quick screening instrument for the detection of potential sexual addiction. Answer each of the questions with a yes or no.

1. Do you often find yourself preoccupied with sexual thoughts? [**Preoccupied**]

    Yes   No

2. Do you hide some of your sexual behavior from others? [**Ashamed**]

    Yes   No

3. Have you ever sought help for sexual behavior you did not like? [**Treatment**]

    Yes   No

4. Has anyone been hurt emotionally because of your sexual behavior? [**Hurt others**]

    Yes   No

5. Do you feel controlled by your sexual desire? [**Out of control**]

    Yes   No

6. When you have sex (masturbation or sex with another), do you feel depressed afterward? [**Sad**]

    Yes   No

If you answered "yes" to three or more of these questions, your sexual behavior might be problematic. During your recovery, you will want to address both your sex/love addiction and your Internet addiction. Seek help from someone who is qualified to treat sex addiction.

What follows is a checklist of the criteria for sexual anorexia. Whether you meet the criteria for sexual addiction or for being sexually anorexic, always seek help from someone qualified to treat your Internet addiction as well as your intimacy disorder.

- ☐ Recurrent pattern of resistance or aversion to any sexual activity, initiative, or behavior
- ☐ Persistent aversion to sexual contact even though it is self-destructive or harmful to relationships
- ☐ Extreme efforts to avoid sexual contact or attention, including self-mutilation, distortions of body appearance or apparel, and aversive behavior
- ☐ Rigid, judgmental attitudes toward personal sexuality and sexuality of others
- ☐ Extreme shame and self-loathing about sexual experiences, body perceptions, and sexual attributes
- ☐ Sexual aversion affects work, hobbies, friends, family, and primary relationship
- ☐ Preoccupation and obsession with avoiding sexual contact and with sexual intentions of others
- ☐ Despair about sexual adequacy and functioning
- ☐ Avoiding intimacy and relationships because of fear of sexual contact
- ☐ Distress, anxiety, restlessness, or irritability because of sexual contact or potential sexual contact

In conclusion, we live in a world where the lines of fantasy and reality are often blurred. It can be confusing and you might not even be aware that you are living in a world based on fantasy. That's why we created the exercises in this chapter. While doing the exercises, you may have discovered you have an intimacy disorder as well as an Internet addiction. It is common for the two problems to happen at the same time. Recovery from both is possible when you accept the need to heal from both. Dealing with one without dealing with the other, however, can lead you away from recovery in the long run. This is because the arousal templates for both are usually comingled.

Beliefs about Men and Women

Directions: There are a lot of Internet/gaming users that have given up on the idea of ever having a long-term relationship. They hold negative beliefs about others, like the belief that all women are cold bitches or that all men are stupid and irresponsible and only want sex.

Below, list all the beliefs you have about men and women:

_____

_____

_____

_____

_____

Write about how these beliefs may have fed your addiction and could become triggering to you in the future.

_____

_____

_____

_____

What beliefs do you hold that you can now identify as possibly untrue but to which you still react emotionally?

Belief One:

_____

_____

_____

_____

What would be a healthier belief?

_____

_____

_____

Belief Two:

_____

_____

_____

_____

What would be a healthier belief?

_____

_____

_____

_____

_____

Belief Three:

_____

_____

_____

_____

What would be a healthier belief?

_____

_____

_____

_____

Belief Four:

_____

_____

_____

_____

What would be a healthier belief?

_____

_____

_____

_____

Belief Five:

_____

_____

_____

_____

What would be a healthier belief?

_____

_____

_____

_____

Finding the Messages in Your Internet Fantasies

In *Harry Potter and the Sorcerer's Stone,* Harry's parents die while protecting him from the evil wizard Voldemort. Eventually, Harry discovers the Mirror of Erised. As he gazes in this mirror, he sees his parents looking back at him with love and approval. Being able to continue doing this becomes Harry's most ardent wish. He keeps revisiting the mirror and shows it to his friend Ron. When Ron gazes in the mirror, however, he sees himself as successful and stepping out of the shadow of his brothers—*his* most ardent wish. Albus Dumbledore, Headmaster of Hogwarts, the school that Harry and Ron attend, learns that the boys have found the mirror and intervenes. He explains that the mirror reflects your deepest desire (*Erised* is the reverse of *desire*). He further tells Ron and Harry that people have literally been captured by the mirror and unable to leave it.

This story about the Mirror of Esired illustrates how living in fantasy falls far short of living in reality. As the story unfolds, Ron is fundamentally better off creating his achievements. In Harry's case, it is impossible to make up for the wound of the loss of his parents. To use the words of Carl Jung, this is Harry's "legitimate suffering." Harry's loss deepens his understanding of the world and strengthens his determination to do well.

We have many stories about the illusions involved in our ardent wishes. The holodeck depicted in the *Star Trek* series of films and television shows was a device that brought fantasies to life, creating a world of three-dimensional images and unfolding events that seemed real. Those who sought their heart's desire there could end up with holo-addiction—an ardent desire to live in their fantasy world.

More than any other vehicle for obsession, the Internet is the Mirror of Erised. Almost any ardent desire can be found therein. Finding what you have always been searching for becomes a way to dissociate from who you really are and what you must do. Accessing the unresolved is the portal through which you can live in obsession versus reality.

Cravings as Communication

Like Harry Potter and the Mirror of Erised, we can lose ourselves in fantasy and miss the core issues of the self that must be addressed. Gazing at the fantasy is like pouring water into a bottomless glass. It never fills.

In this way, our addiction is a kind of ally, protecting us from some truth we wish not to face. Almost always, addiction's presence means that some unbearable truth resides within. This is also why addictions frequently present themselves in different forms and combinations. If we resolve one addiction, others surface to keep that truth obscured.

Thus, cravings are communications that the self is in distress at a deep level. True recovery will not be achieved until the wounds are addressed. Nor will any amount of abstinence take away the fundamental obsession until the hurt is understood and resolved.

Mirror of Desire

Directions: Imagine you have a mirror in which you can see that which you want the most. Make a list of what you would see in that mirror. Be honest with yourself.

One way to approach this exercise is to ask what you would give up everything for—those things for which you would trade your soul. All of us have them. They are important to acknowledge as part of your healing.

Start now by listing your most ardent desires. They may be relational, sexual, professional, or something else. What scenes would appear in your mirror? Please describe them below.

_____

_____

_____

_____

_____

_____

_____

Now make a list of your ideal sexual fantasies. These are the fantasies that are the most powerful in your life. Gazing in your mirror, what sexual fantasies would appear?

_____

_____

_____

_____

_____

_____

_____

_____

Finally, reflect on themes that emerge. Are they reflected in your Internet use? Talk with your therapist, sponsor, and recovery support people about this.

_____

_____

_____

_____

_____

_____

_____

_____

_____

_____

_____

The Wounds that Drive Your Desires

Directions: Harry Potter gazed in the mirror that brought him relief from grieving over his parent's deaths. In a similar way, addictive behavior "protects" us from the pain of reality. In their woundedness, users turn to behaviors that help them cope. Behind damaged coping and addictive focusing are core experiences of pain.

Perhaps they came from early wounds or experiences in your life. Or they could present a difficult truth about you that has been too painful to face. List these drivers of your Internet/gaming use:

_____

_____

_____

_____

_____

_____

_____

What have been the costs of not acknowledging these wounds? Include both addictive and non-addictive costs.

_____

_____

_____

_____

_____

_____

      Reflect on what steps you could take to heal from those experiences that have supported dysfunction and addiction in your life.

_____

_____

_____

_____

_____

_____

_____

_____

_____

_____

_____

When it comes to discovering what drives your addictive behavior, knowledge is power. After completing all the exercises in this chapter, you now have some powerful knowledge that can help you recognize what triggers your addictive behavior. You can now use that knowledge to make better decisions. How will you do that? By taking that first step.

Chapter 6

What Is a First Step?
Accepting the Problem

Addictions have a great deal in common, but different addictions are also unique in some ways. Appendix A compares the Twelve Steps and Principles of Internet and Technology Addicts Anonymous (ITAA) to the Twelve Steps of Alcoholics Anonymous (AA), a program started decades ago and one that has helped millions of people get better.

   We've found that individuals in recovery for Internet addiction and gaming disorder who are willing to take the Twelve Steps seriously and who do the real work of those steps get better. Why? Because we all need to be part of a community that "gets" who we are, what our struggles are, and to whom we can turn to for support.

   The Twelve Steps teach us how to make profound changes in our lives. The spirit of these principles is best captured in the Serenity Prayer:

God grant me the serenity
to accept the things I cannot change;
courage to change the things I can;
and wisdom to know the difference.

   Addictions draw power from shame. The internal acceptance of the Serenity Prayer ideas may help reduce anxiety dramatically. The First Step of ITAA captures this principle. It reads:

We admitted we were powerless over our addiction—that our lives had become unmanageable.

   People who do a First Step usually learn the following lessons:

- You must accept totally that you have a problem.

- There are things that you cannot control by yourself.

- To be successful in recovery, you have to ask for support from others.

- In recovery, you must focus on what you *can* do.

- In recovery, you must give up secrets and pretending to be something you are not.

- Addictive behaviors will continue until you truly apply these lessons.

The following exercises will help you prepare for a First Step. These tasks may be difficult, but you must complete them as honestly and thoroughly as you can. Don't forget to ask for support. A therapist, your therapy group, and people in your Twelve Step group (if you choose to be in one) can be wonderful resources. So, whenever you feel shame or get frustrated, reach out to someone and ask for help. Recovery starts with that First Step.

Your Internet Addiction History

Directions: Respond to the following questions as best you can. If it helps, go back to Chapter 1 to jog your memory. You may find it helpful to create a timeline to identify how your addiction progressed over time. Place key events on your timeline and notate when your addictive behavior increased or decreased.

1. How did your dependence on the Internet, screen use, or gaming begin (that is, how did your online behavior help you to cope; how did you avoid offline stressors and activities by going to your screens)?

   _____

   _____

2. What led to your awareness that this is a major problem for you?

   _____

   _____

3. What was going on in your life when your use started spiraling out of control? Were there major stressors (relationship strife, parental or sibling addiction, a move, abuse or neglect, illness or injury, bullying at school, etc.)?

   _____

   _____

   _____

   _____

4. Describe the period of time you believe your Internet or video gaming dependence was firmly established (when your screen preoccupation really interfered with your life).

_____

_____

_____

_____

5. Describe how you justified your use, making it OK to continue what you were doing.

_____

_____

_____

_____

6. Were there periods during your life in which your screen use or gaming suddenly escalated in terms of frequency or types of online behavior?

    Circle or highlight one: Yes   No

    If yes, at what ages (for example, 15–18, 22–24, 30)?

_____

_____

7. Was there a seasonal (spring, summer, fall, winter) pattern in your online use?

    Circle or highlight one: Yes   No

    If yes, please specify:

8. What were some critical events during these periods of increased use?

_____

_____

_____

_____

9. At what ages do you believe your Internet, screen use, or gaming was at its highest level?

_____

10. What were some critical events that took place when your Internet, screen use, or gaming was at its highest level?

_____

_____

_____

_____

11. Were there periods during your life when your digital use de-escalated (was less intense or was controlled)?

Circle or highlight one: Yes   No

If yes, at what ages?

_____

12. What were some critical events that preceded this de-escalation or that occurred during it?

_____

_____

_____

_____

_____

13. Were there periods when it seemed that you had no offline life?

Circle or highlight one: Yes   No

If yes, at what ages or periods in your life?

_____

14. What were some critical events during these periods?

_____

_____

_____

_____

_____

15. Are you currently working on limiting other problematic behaviors, or are you currently in recovery for any other addiction?

Circle or highlight one: Yes   No

Check all that apply below:

_____   alcohol or other drugs
_____   addiction to sex, porn, or romance/love
_____   codependency
_____   eating disorders (binge eating, anorexia, bulimia)
_____   nicotine/tobacco/vaping addiction
_____   caffeine abuse or addiction
_____   compulsive gambling
_____   compulsive spending
_____   compulsive work
_____   other, specify: _____

16. Do you engage in some of the behaviors listed above but choose not to work on them?

Circle or highlight one: Yes   No

If so, which ones?

_____

What keeps you from working on these behaviors?

_____

_____

_____

_____

17. How have other addictions (if any) affected your Internet, screen, or gaming use?

_____

_____

_____

_____

_____

_____

_____

_____

_____

_____

_____

Powerlessness Inventory

Directions: Being powerless means you are unable to stop your behavior despite obvious negative consequences. For example: "I knew that if I missed one more assignment, I was going to be kicked out of the course and would probably lose my scholarship. I might even be kicked out of college altogether. Yet I stayed up playing all that night, didn't do the assignment, and didn't show up for class the next day." If you need more space to write, continue in your journal.

1. _____

_____

2. _____

_____

3. _____

_____

4. _____

_____

5. _____

_____

Go back and circle examples that have happened in the last 10 days. Then, circle examples that have happened in the last 30 days. After you've done that, stop and share what you've written with one of your support people. This isn't easy stuff to think and write about, so be kind to yourself. Sharing this makes it easier.

Unmanageability Inventory

Directions: Unmanageability means that your behavior has created chaos and damage in your life. For example: "I got caught stealing from my parents so I could buy gear for my game." List as many examples as you can that show how your life and your digital media use (e.g., Internet, screens, gaming, etc.) have become unmanageable. If you need ideas, return to chapter 1 and review your list of consequences. If you need more space to write, continue in your journal.

After you have completed your list, consider the events that felt the most unmanageable to you. These are usually the most recent events. Circle or highlight your most recent examples of unmanageability.

When you finish this exercise, stop and talk to your support network before moving on in this workbook. You deserve support.

1. _____

_____

2. _____

_____

3. _____

_____

4. _____

_____

5. _____

_____

Financial Costs

If you're young and dependent on your family for financial support, you may not be aware of the financial costs of your behavior. However, we predict that if you think about this closely, you'll see that no matter how young you are, there have been costs. We've worked with quite a few people who have spent huge sums on gear, new equipment, new games, etc., often on a credit card which they could not pay off, or by stealing from their parents or partners through unauthorized use of their credit cards. Keep in mind that using a line of credit belonging to your parents and made available to you for specific non-gaming expenses (like education) is considered to be unauthorized use. Additionally, think about the costs to those who were supporting you while you gamed, and you did not get or hold a job and contribute to the expenses of your existence. What about all the money your family may have spent on tuition at a school you flunked out of? What about losing a scholarship? These are costs to be reckoned with, too. Perhaps you've had medical problems because of your unhealthy lifestyle? Have you gotten into legal problems, which are often costly? Did you have to go through a divorce as a result of your problematic use? Did you lose a job because of it? A home? The list of potential financial ramifications for problematic use is long.

Make a list of all the financial costs that you or your family have paid as a result of your addictive behavior. Estimate the actual monetary value for each.

What you and others went through because of your problematic use, i.e., divorce, lost job, lost home	How much it cost

What you and others went through because of your problematic use, i.e., divorce, lost job, lost home	How much it cost

Add up the total dollar cost here: $ _____

What insights or reflections do you have now that you have an approximate cost of your addictive behavior? If that money were available to you today, what would you be able to do with it? Record your thoughts here:

_____

_____

_____

_____

_____

_____

_____

_____

_____

Denial and Delusion Inventory

Directions: Give five examples of *denial* about your spending on gaming, gambling, porn, etc. For example: "My parents have lots of money, so using their credit card for this item makes no difference to them," or "What is money for if not to have fun?"

1. _____

   _____

2. _____

   _____

3. _____

   _____

4. _____

   _____

5. _____

   _____

Now give five examples of *delusion* (rationalization and justification) about your spending. For example: "My parents are so ignorant and unreasonable. They give me a hard time about not working, but I'm on my way to becoming a pro gamer making a good living."

1. _____

   _____

2. _____

_____

3. _____

_____

4. _____

_____

5. _____

_____

Record your reactions to your denial and delusions about the financial costs of your actions. Start with your thoughts and then record your feelings.

Thoughts: For example: "What was I thinking?"

_____

_____

_____

_____

Feelings: For example: "I feel guilty."

_____

_____

_____

_____

Five Worst Moments

Directions: List your five worst moments related to your problematic use. Think of events that were the most painful or catastrophic. For each event, record the feelings you had then and the feelings you have now as you look back on these moments.

1. Worst moment: _____

_____

Feelings then: _____

Feelings now: _____

2. Worst moment: _____

_____

Feelings then: _____

Feelings now: _____

3. Worst moment: _____

_____

Feelings then: _____

Feelings now: _____

4. Worst moment: _____

_____

Feelings then: _____

Feelings now: _____

5. Worst moment: _____

_____

Feelings then: _____

Feelings now: _____

Now that you have completed the list, rank order the worst moments by putting a "1" next to the very worst, a "2" next to the second worst, and so on. Continue until you have ranked all five. This will help you focus on what you will share in your First Step process.

Putting It All Together

Directions: It's now time to write a narrative of your life. You will write about how all the important things in your life formed who you are today. Include when you began using technology, your family's use of technology, your peers, etc. If you want to add a drawing, feel free to do so. This is an exercise to do in your journal.

Congratulations! Now that you've put all of the pieces of your story together, it's time to share it with others. First, share it with people that you know and those who have a deep understanding of your struggles. This will probably be your therapist, members of your therapy and Twelve Step group, and your sponsor. As time goes by, you may decide to share it with others that you want to get closer to. But choose these people wisely. This is not information to be shared lightly. As you feel less and less shame from sharing your story with others, you will find it becomes easier to share and talk about your story. The loss of shame is one of the great gifts of therapy and the Twelve Step process. Being vulnerable is a strong and courageous act.

If you are working with a sponsor, this person may ask you to go over aspects of your story with particular emphasis in certain difficult areas. Asking you to work on it more is normal. They are supporting and pushing you because getting to the point of complete acceptance is the way forward, the way for you to meet your deepest needs for health.

Ultimately, through the whole process of 12-step work, you will be pushed to look deeply at yourself and your behavior. Your first step will be your first go at the following:

- No excuses or explanations (in other words, acknowledge your behavior without minimizing or blaming others).

- A clear understanding of powerlessness, with good examples of efforts to stop.

- A clear understanding of unmanageability, with good examples of consequences.

- Knowledge of your own addictive system.

- Knowledge of how your behavior fits the criteria for addiction.

- The worst moments expressed and the secrets exposed.

- Taking full responsibility for actions.

- A range of feelings expressed.

- Feelings are appropriate for the events reported.

- Acknowledgement of suffering you've caused, including grief, pain, sorrow, and remorse.

- Ownership of loneliness.

- A commitment to do whatever it takes to change.

Quite often, people get confused about how one can be powerless and still take responsibility. A paradox does exist here, but it untangles if you remember this: *Alone you are powerless. You were not able to stop your behavior. With support you* *can.* You did the behavior. No one else is responsible for it. Now, by knowing what you know, you have a responsibility to use the tools you have and to get the support you need so that you can change.

Preventing Self-Sabotage

The "Big Book" of Alcoholics Anonymous describes addiction as "cunning, baffling, and powerful." This is an apt description. Because of this, people with addictions often attempt to sabotage their First Step. There are several things that might happen:

- You may be tempted to engage in escapist or addictive screen use or gaming, even in some minor way.
- You may want to keep a secret or protect someone.
- You may want to procrastinate on your First Step.
- You may find distractions and things to upset or distract you.
- You may find fault with your group, your therapist, or your treatment program.
- You may find or create a family crisis.
- You may find yourself craving to act on your other addictions.
- You may find yourself mired in self-hatred and self-loathing.
- You may deny the significance of the problems you are facing.
- You may deny that your problems relate to your thinking. You may blame your problems entirely on feeling depressed or anxious.

In other words, part of you may prompt you to stay loyal to your old behaviors. Yet if you persevere, you'll find that the First Step teaches a new and more conscious way of life. Anxiety and depression may become your guide, rather than your enemy. You will learn that change is the substance of life and that the unknown is for each of us. That which used to hold you back will become an extraordinary source of wisdom. You'll still face troubles of all sorts in your life, but you will become effective at handling them with healthy tools that you learn through the recovery process. You will understand how to cope with day-to-day problems that all functional adults (and young adults) must face. You will forge new bonds and be respected for how you handle yourself. No matter how big the fear or challenge, you will have a sense of peace about it.

Chapter 7

Responding to Change and Crisis: You Need to Change the Way You Think

Long-lasting change is hard. Think about how many years you've been steeped in your bad habits. It's going to take time to develop new habits that will keep you on a healthy life path. You've already got a start on that path: You've gotten this far in the workbook, you're working with a therapist, perhaps you've been in a treatment program, etc. Whatever you're doing, it's the beginning of a lifelong journey toward becoming the healthy, happy, and productive person that you have the potential to be. Staying on that path requires changing your behavior, beliefs, and thought patterns. The following exercises are designed to help you with that. We know from experience that truly believing you can change is often hard. So, as you move forward in this chapter, we want you to begin by embracing the following beliefs.

- **For the time being, you may not be able to trust your own perceptions.** You will have to trust the perceptions of others who are actively supporting you, even as mistaken and unpleasant as you believe them to be.

- **For the time being, you will have to trust that you have been harmed far more than you know.** You must also remember that time and recovery can work wonders in repairing this harm and helping you become the person you were meant to be.

- **For the time being, you must remember that addictive behaviors undermine reality.** You need to believe that it is critical to pursue a healthier life. The only way out of suffering is to tell those who are supporting you what has happened. Then they can support you in reclaiming greater health and wellness. You must do this without minimizing or omitting awkward details. You may not make private deals with yourself about holding things back. Anything less than full disclosure lowers the probability of your recovery.

- **For the time being, you must allow people to care for you.** Do this even if you do not feel that you deserve anyone's love and care. You are important, valued, and appreciated in ways that are hard to accept right now. This means you must follow through on what is asked of you; you must surrender control of your life to those who can care about you and your happiness.

Most people at this point are facing problems and challenges that resulted from their addictive behavior: academic failure, lost relationships, severe conflict with family, etc. The list may seem endless, and it can feel overwhelming. Recovery teaches that the best way to deal with this is to get support and to keep things simple. For starters, you can use smart goals to break up tasks into smaller parts that can be tackled one at a time, one day at a time.

S.M.A.R.T. GOALS (Peter Drucker)

Specific _____

      (e.g., I'd like to finish my degree.)

Measurable _____

      (e.g., I will sign up for two classes each semester.)

Attainable _____

      (e.g., I will stop by campus, review the course list, and select two courses.)

Relevant _____

      (e.g., Earning my degree will help me get a higher paying job.)

Time-Based _____

      (e.g., I will enroll in two classes by the end of this month.)

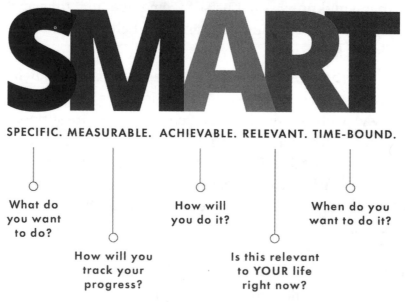

WHAT ARE SMART GOALS?

SMART

SPECIFIC. MEASURABLE. ACHIEVABLE. RELEVANT. TIME-BOUND.

What do you want to do?

How will you track your progress?

How will you do it?

Is this relevant to YOUR life right now?

When do you want to do it?

Current Problem List

Directions: This exercise will help you prepare for making a damage control plan. Begin by making a list of the problems you are currently facing. You may wish to refer to Exercise 1.1, the Problem List you made in chapter 1. This new list, however, should focus on your current problems, such as unemployment, school failure, poor health, or homelessness.

1. _____

_____

_____

2. _____

_____

_____

3. _____

_____

_____

4. _____

_____

_____

5. _____

_____

_____

6. _____

_____

_____

7. _____

_____

_____

8. _____

_____

_____

Damage Control Worksheets

The following Damage Control Worksheets encourage you to think through each of the problems you just listed in an organized and logical way. You will find that this way of thinking through problems is helpful when things feel chaotic and overwhelming. You can also use these tools as normal life difficulties arise.

For each problem that you list on a Damage Control Worksheet, you will be asked to write the following:

- **Best possible outcome:** Imagine that you could produce the result that you want most of all. What would that result be?

- **Minimum acceptable outcome:** Of all the results that you could produce, what is the least desirable one that you can still accept?

- **Possible solutions:** Gather all the solutions that you and the people in your support system suggest. List each solution, no matter how far-fetched it may seem.

- **Best solution:** From your list of possible solutions, choose and combine ideas to arrive at the most desirable one that you can actually produce.

- **Action steps with target dates:** What concrete actions are required to produce your best solution? By what date will you take each step?

- **Support needed:** What do you need in order to take these action steps? Who do you need to help you?

Use one Damage Control Worksheet for each problem. If you need more space (and many people do), simply continue the exercise in your journal.

As you carefully plan out your action steps and include the support you need, the tasks will seem more doable. Using this damage control process will help you build support systems and deal with problems in ways that can continue to help you throughout your recovery.

Damage Control Worksheet 1

Directions: See previous page.

Example Problem: I failed out of college. My major was biology and my plan was to become a doctor. Now my chances of getting into med school seem to be nil.

Your Problem:

_____

_____

_____

_____

Example Best Possible Outcome: If they accept me back and I can retake my failed courses to get my GPA into a good place, then I can still get into med school.

Your Best Possible Outcome:

_____

_____

_____

_____

Example Minimum Acceptable Outcome: I may have to go to another school and start all over, perhaps even taking out student loans if my parents aren't willing to support my schooling any longer. This will be a setback, but if I do well, I may still be able to go to med school. If not med school, then I could switch to bioengineering for a good job right out of college.

Your Minimum Acceptable Outcome:

_____

_____

_____

_____

Your Possible Solutions:

1. Example: Earn my parents' trust in hopes they will support me in college again.

_____

_____

2. Example: Convince the university to take me back.

_____

_____

3. Example: Apply to other schools that would allow me to get where I want to go.

_____

_____

4. _____

_____

5. _____

_____

6. _____

_____

7. _____

_____

8. _____

_____

Your Best Solution:

Example: My university accepts me back, allows me to pursue biology again, and my parents agree to support me financially.

_____

_____

_____

_____

Your Action Steps:

Action Step 1 – Example: Talk to parents.

_____

Date taken by – Example: Dec 15

_____

Action Step 2 – Example: Talk to the admissions office at _____ to find out what I need to do to be accepted back into the U.

_____

_____

Date taken by – Example: Dec 20

_____

Action Step 3 – Example: Ask my doctor to write a letter on my behalf.

_____

_____

Date taken by – Example: TBD based on the timeline given by the university.

_____

Action Step 4 – Example: Write an essay for the university explaining what happened, my recovery, and why they should take a chance on me again.

_____

_____

Date taken by – Example: Jan _____

Support Needed – Example: _____

1. Plan with my therapist how to talk with my parents.
2. Let my recovery group know what I'm trying to do and check in with them before and after my conversation with parents.
3. Do the same with talking to the admissions office.
4. Ask my therapist and recovery group to read over and comment on what I write in my essay.

_____

_____

_____

_____

Damage Control Worksheet 2

Problem:

_____

_____

_____

_____

Best Possible Outcome:

_____

_____

_____

_____

Minimum Acceptable Outcome:

_____

_____

_____

_____

Possible Solutions:

1. _____

_____

2. _____

   _____

3. _____

   _____

4. _____

   _____

5. _____

   _____

6. _____

   _____

7. _____

   _____

8. _____

   _____

Best Solution:

_____

_____

_____

_____

_____

Action Steps:

1. _____

_____

Date taken by: _____

2. _____

_____

Date taken by: _____

3. _____

_____

Date taken by: _____

4. _____

_____

Date taken by: _____

5. _____

_____

Date taken by: _____

Support Needed:

_____

_____

_____

_____

Facing Internet Technology and Gaming Addiction

Damage Control Worksheet 3

Problem:

_____

_____

_____

_____

Best Possible Outcome:

_____

_____

_____

_____

Minimum Acceptable Outcome:

_____

_____

_____

_____

Possible Solutions:

1. _____

_____

$\longrightarrow$

2. _____

_____

3. _____

_____

4. _____

_____

5. _____

_____

6. _____

_____

7. _____

_____

8. _____

_____

Best Solution:

_____

_____

_____

_____

_____

Action Steps:

1. _____

_____

Date taken by: _____

2. _____

_____

Date taken by: _____

3. _____

_____

Date taken by: _____

4. _____

_____

Date taken by: _____

5. _____

_____

Date taken by: _____

Support Needed:

_____

_____

_____

_____

It is not easy to face reality when you've messed up. And let's face it, if you're working this workbook, you've messed up in some major way or another. However, as the exercises above have hopefully taught you, once you make a realistic assessment of the harm you've experienced and begin to think constructively about how to manage the situations you face, you begin to see there are ways to contain and repair the damage.

As you begin to take steps toward making long-lasting behavior changes in your life, something amazing happens. You begin to realize all the potential you have and what you've been missing out on because of your addictive behavior. That feeling is pretty amazing! Savor it.

Chapter 8

Sobriety—It's a Hero's Journey

In one of the beginning scenes of J. R. R. Tolkien's great epic, *Lord of the Rings*, the wizard Gandalf challenges the hobbit Frodo to bring peace to the land by taking a magic ring to the land of Mordor where it can be destroyed. The destruction of the ring is the key to freedom from the tyranny of the evil magician Sauron. Gandalf holds out the ring for Frodo to accept the quest.

Frodo feels a penetrating chill, which he immediately knows has been sent by Sauron to distract him from accepting the challenge. This evil is designed to paralyze Frodo and render him incapable of responding to Gandalf.

In response, Frodo musters all the courage he can and slowly raises his hand to accept the ring. He hears his own voice, though it seems far away. He says to Gandalf, "I will take the ring though I do not know the way." Thus begins Frodo's great quest.

All the great stories of human courage start with the hero not knowing how to achieve his or her task but starting anyway. So it is with recovery. The people who succeed in recovery are the ones who start even though they do not know the way. Along the path, they find out that part of the benefit of setting out on a quest is what they learn as they make their journey. That said, the point here is that they start on their quest and simply trust that it will take them someplace difficult to reach but worthwhile.

Addiction is a Boundary Problem

People in recovery typically start out with poor boundaries. As addicts, they want whatever it is that they think will make them feel good, bring relief, or distract them, and they want it NOW. Often, their poor boundaries around their behavior are learned from their family, which had poor boundaries or boundaries that were easy to work around.

For many addicts, making the decision to be free of addictive behavior is the first time they've set a meaningful boundary. Having a clear statement about abstinence allows them to start the journey of knowing what they value, what they need, what they want out of life—in other words, to know who they are.

We've met many "Mr. Nice Guys" in our work with Internet and video game addiction. These people tend to say what they think others want to hear (or they stay silent) rather than speaking their thoughts, feelings, and needs, and dealing with whatever that brings. Mr. Nice Guys don't have healthy boundaries.

Learning to set limits is both a revelation and a revolution in a recovering person's life. A clear sense of what matters to them now governs their life. Self-respect returns. A new toughness emerges that gains the respect of others. Ironically, this toughness brings a sense of peace never before experienced.

For you, the addictive behaviors which have kept you so driven have a power of their own. As a result, it's likely that all the promises you made to yourself to set boundaries failed. Part of recovery is to accept that even the most disciplined people are powerless to control their behavior by themselves when they have an addiction. Learning to have healthy boundaries is a necessary part of becoming a healthy, well-balanced human being. Finding support while you clarify and strengthen your boundaries is part of the recovery process.

Knowing what you feel, what you value, what you need—these are essential elements to develop within yourself as you learn how to set healthy boundaries with self and others. When you know yourself well, you can ask for what you want or need, and you can accept when others say yes or no. When you know yourself well, you can honestly say yes or no to what others ask of you, rather than automatically saying yes to please them or automatically saying no out of mistrust or anxiety. Once you know and accept yourself, it will become clear to you where you start and stop. Committing to recovery is a boundary based on you knowing what the first step is to becoming healthy. When you don't allow anything or anyone to stop you from doing what you know you need, you are showing a strong boundary. A boundary collapse is what happens when you've set a boundary but do not maintain it. Learning what your boundaries are and developing the strength to maintain them happens over time and through recovery. Be patient with yourself.

Write about times that you wanted to speak up and ask for what you needed but did not, or you wanted to say "no" but instead said "yes."

_____

_____

_____

_____

_____

How to Avoid Boundary Failure

Directions: Boundaries succeed and fail for the following reasons. Read the descriptions and then write your answers when prompted.

1. Underachievement and Overachievement

Most of the people with gaming disorder that we have worked with over the years have been very competitive. The games they play are highly competitive (MOBAs, MMORPGs, first-person shooters, etc.), and they have often achieved high rankings in those games. (This is not always true, of course. Some play for other reasons, like for the social aspect of the games). Quite often, these players are perfectionists both in-game and offline. Since a person can get closer to perfection in a game than in the real world, we've seen a tendency for gamers to put their energies into gaming and procrastinate or never complete the offline tasks required by school or work. The net result is increasing failure in day-to-day living and overinvestment in gaming. Thus, paradoxically, overachievement in the cyber-world leads to underachievement in overall living.

As failures in school, work, and relationships pile up, self-esteem takes a beating. This will fuel further investment in the areas of success that boost self-esteem — the Internet, gaming, and screen time. And so it goes, round and round, in a downward spiral until a person is clinging desperately to their one source of comfort and achievement, harboring, but hiding from, an increasing sense of failure and shame.

In this section, write about ways in which you overachieved in some areas while underachieving in others. Next to each topic, circle whether you overachieved or underachieved in that area and then explain how. You can use your journal to expand upon your answers.

- **School** (circle one):   **Overachievement**   **Underachievement**

_____

_____

_____

_____

- **Paid Work** (circle one): **Overachievement**   **Underachievement**

_____

_____

_____

_____

- **Hobbies** (circle one): **Overachievement**   **Underachievement**

_____

_____

_____

_____

- **Sports/Fitness** (circle one): **Overachievement**   **Underachievement**

_____

_____

_____

_____

- **Friendships/Romantic Relationships** (circle one):
  Overachievement   **Underachievement**

_____

_____

_____

_____

- **Other**

_____

_____

_____

_____

2. Self-Esteem

Low self-esteem can develop for many reasons. It typically develops as the result of unhealthy dynamics in childhood, such as parents abusing or neglecting a child. Children who experience this tend to have a falsely low sense of self-worth. Conversely, parents who over-attend to a child, praising too much and inappropriately, doing too much, not asking enough, etc., will foster a sense of entitlement, over-inflated self-esteem (grandiosity), and egocentricity. These children typically can have a falsely high or low sense of self-worth—high because they believe they are entitled, low because they know, on some level, that they have not earned what they have. Children from either side of this coin become adults who do not know how to evaluate themselves realistically, knowing their faults and their strengths. Generally, it is difficult for them to accept and love themselves as worthy but imperfect human beings. The Internet can become the place where these individuals, believing themselves either too special or not special enough, can turn for pleasure, escape, and a narrow, fragile kind of self-esteem based on their online prowess and prestige.

Being either self-absorbed or filled with shame causes the same result—a distorted picture of your place in the universe. In recovery, it is important to develop an appreciation for yourself that is realistic, not inflated or deflated.

Take some time to sort through these feelings:

- Make a list of things, big or small, that you have done that you feel genuinely proud of. We are not asking for achievements in your online world here, only achievements in your offline life.

_____

_____

_____

_____

_____

- Make a list of times when you have talked yourself into some sort of failure (for example, you talked yourself out of asking someone you liked out for a date).

_____

_____

_____

_____

- Make a list of events when your preoccupation with yourself hurt those you care about.

_____

_____

_____

_____

- Considering these lists, make another quick list of your strengths and limitations.

Strengths _____

_____

_____

_____

_____

Limitations _____

_____

_____

_____

_____

_____

We strongly suggest that you learn about using affirmations as part of your healing process. Essentially, affirmations help reprogram your brain so that you can accept the love-worthy person you are. The path out of self-hatred is to find a way to affirm yourself from within so you have a realistic and confident sense of yourself. Affirmations are aspiration, but they should be positively stated, as if they are already true. Here are a few examples:

I am loveable just as I am.

I grow healthier when I make mistakes and learn from them.

Write one or two affirmations that, when you come to believe them, will help you to feel good about yourself:

_____

_____

3. Accountability

People often resist being accountable. They are more interested in doing what they want, no matter how irresponsible it is. They don't want others to find out and hold them accountable. There are many paths that can lead to this irresponsibility. Perhaps it started young because of how rigid or controlling their family was, so they rebelled or became defiant. It might have started because their parents were too permissive and they were not required to behave responsibly. It might have happened because their parents didn't know what to do when faced with raising a child in the digital age and ended up being ineffective and inconsistent. Perhaps their parents modeled irresponsibility in their own behavior. Whatever the reason, the net result is that many people, especially those with addictions, struggle to be accountable and responsible.

There is much research that tells us that, among other important things, good parents are good role models for their kids, and this includes admitting their mistakes to their children. Such children grow up knowing that it is OK to be imperfect, so they are not afraid to be held and to hold themselves accountable for their mistakes.

Saying "no" is a first step in learning to set a boundary for oneself. We know that healthy parents provide lots of love along with firm, clear, consistent limits, while at the same time listening and respecting the child's "no" and being willing to negotiate when appropriate. We have seen that it is particularly hard to raise children in the digital age. It is difficult to set appropriate boundaries and manage to effectively keep household tech use within normal, healthy limits because the world is changing so rapidly that most parents are not prepared to understand, let alone deal with its impact on their children. And parents are impacted themselves. Many are wedded to their devices just as much as their kids.

The net result is that many people miss core lessons about accountability. Typically, they do not do what they say they will. They do not admit their mistakes. They do not let anyone know what they really do with their time, their money, or their actions. They keep secrets.

Others are accountable in appearance only. In business, the phrase is "keeping a separate set of books"—one for show and one that is kept secret. There are many young adults who, especially in high school, were able to precariously keep it together, only to fail later. They were smart enough to do well academically so their parents left them alone, but secretly, they were gaming excessively, stealing money for their games, spending hours on forbidden porn, etc. No one was holding them accountable because they kept their secrets well.

Recovery works only if there is total accountability. Your group, your therapist, and your sponsor become important links to accountability. Keeping secrets from them simply will not work. You need to have people in your life who know and accept you, and who will challenge you.

Write a paragraph here about how you got around rules and what the consequences were when you were caught.

_____

_____

_____

_____

_____

_____

_____

_____

What lessons do you think you learned from this?

_____

_____

_____

_____

_____

_____

_____

_____

4. Self-Care

Self-care involves many things. It means living a well-balanced life, a life with enough sleep, eating healthy food, socializing with healthy people, getting adequate exercise, staying clean and well-groomed, keeping your living space clean. It also means taking time to be mindful of all there is to be thankful for, like being able to call on your support network when you need it.

With problematic tech use, there is a tendency to neglect one or more important areas of self-care. Some tech addicts develop extensive dental problems from not brushing their teeth, some are overweight from lack of exercise and eating unhealthy food, some smell bad because they rarely bathe, and so forth. There can be many reasons for this self-neglect. Below we present some possibilities to think about. See if anything applies to you.

Childhood neglect and abuse are common among those with addictions. Busy or uncaring parents who do not take the time to help and guide their children through life really are neglecting them. The children who fail to internalize the skills of taking care of themselves are at risk of being exploited by others. Children can learn to neglect their own bodies and welfare. As they grow up, they do not love themselves enough to go the extra length for good self-care. For these people, recovery is difficult because it requires a significant reorientation. They have to take care of themselves to avoid relapse, yet this can be such a hard lesson to learn!

Other people live with parents who do everything for them. Consequently, they do not learn how to do things for themselves, and they expect everything to be done for them. We have seen this in wealthy families in which "nanny kids" have every whim met but still did not feel their parents' love. We have also seen parents of modest means overprotect and cater to their children, who also feel unloved. If there are no real consequences for unhealthy behavior, it can lead to grandiosity and entitlement. No matter what these kids do or do not do, someone rescues them. They may become upset when things are not done for them. They may even be outraged if no one rescues them when they need help. For these individuals, recovery can be a rude awakening to the fact that they must become independent adults, responsible for themselves.

Recovery requires self-care, and you must do it for yourself. Self-care means you do not put yourself in jeopardy. You do the regular things that maintain your health. You floss when you brush your teeth. You consistently exercise. You avoid depletion. You let your friends do kind things for you. You figure out nice things to do for yourself. You take your recovery seriously, let your sponsor help you, and go to meetings. In short, neither neglect nor entitlement work in recovery.

Write about ways you've neglected yourself and ways you recognize that you want/need to take better care of yourself.

_____

_____

_____

_____

Write about ways you would like others to take care of you, relieving you of responsibility for your own happiness and welfare.

_____

_____

_____

_____

5. Conscience

A mentioned earlier, levels of empathy have been declining for the last few decades. This is not surprising to us because other research has shown clearly that many of the things we do on the Internet, such as looking at porn, playing violent video games, trolling, cyber-bullying, and flaming one another in various online forums, all lead to a diminishing of empathy. If you don't care when another person is hurt or in pain, it is easy to not feel guilty about your hurtful behaviors. Add to this the "me first" thinking that is so common in those struggling with addiction and you have a situation where Internet and gaming addicts entering recovery have a lot of ground to cover to develop an effective conscience.

Why is this important?

Because your conscience is your guide. Without it, you have no guide for what is right and what is wrong. You may have an intellectual idea of right and wrong behavior, but without a conscience, you will not _feel_ it.

Some people have no remorse for their behavior even though they have clearly hurt others. In its most extreme cases, we use the term "sociopath" when there is no empathy for victims. Usually, this term is used for criminals. Yet some tech addicts show this quality of no regard for others while in active addiction and even in early recovery. Ultimately, recovery means taking responsibility for your behavior and caring about how it affects both yourself _and others_.

The feeling of shame stems from a deep feeling of being unworthy of love. Guilt, on the other hand, is feeling bad about your behavior. Addicts often feel both.

Part of the pain of addiction for many users is that they have violated their value system and they feel shame. One important part of the addiction cycle is feeling despair after doing behavior they feel shame about. Addicts who are not in recovery then act out further in an effort to blot out the despair. Torturing themselves for behavior that was exploitive or thoughtless adds power to the addictive process. However, if exposure to the online world has let them grow up without any clear sense of what is right or wrong (no clear, strong moral compass), then they may not suffer the remorse that many other people with addiction suffer. If so, then they are someone who has much work to do to fill in that void!

The Twelve Steps will help guide you through a process in which you do all you can to make amends and learn how to make peace with yourself. Sometimes you have to start by clarifying what your values actually are. Many people are not clear about this at the beginning of recovery.

Even though you may not be clear about what you think is of value in human relationships, please have a go at putting some of your ideas down. This is not a lengthy exercise to help you figure out all your values—you'll do that through recovery and therapy—but this is a time to reflect upon how you want to relate to others so that you can feel proud of yourself, rather than ashamed.

_____

_____

_____

_____

_____

6. Realism

People describe a person who is realistic as pragmatic and having common sense. In short, people who learn from and try not to repeat their mistakes. Einstein is commonly credited with saying, "Insanity is doing the same thing over and over and expecting different results." Many people also use this as a definition of addiction. Learning from your mistakes is essential to your mental health. Some people do not develop this ability. Usually, they come from families in which they were not allowed to experience consequences. They never had to figure out that many of their problems were brought on by their own behavior. Recovery, however, is built on common sense. Recovery understands that we do influence our own happiness—and unhappiness.

Sometimes addicts are people who have common sense but choose to ignore it. This is the problem of willfulness. Along with entitlement and grandiosity comes the thought, *I want what I want when I want it, and I don't care about the consequences.*

Problematic digital users are creative, resourceful people who shrewdly figure out how to overcome intrusive reality. Yet sooner or later they have to learn from their mistakes and not rely on their damage-control skills. Recovery brings them to acceptance of reality, both past and present. As you begin this process of returning to reality, take some time to reflect on what (if anything) you have learned from your mistakes.

_____

_____

_____

_____

_____

7. Self-Awareness

The overstimulation, constant distraction, and exhaustion that people with behavioral addictions experience keeps them unaware of their inner experience. Typically, they do not know much about themselves. In part, this is due to the belief that they are unworthy. They may feel so defective that they are uncomfortable being in their own presence. So, they distract themselves with compulsive busyness, filling their lives with so much activity that there is no real interior life. Many report that a fear of being alone was a significant factor in their behavior.

Others will avoid or procrastinate on any activity that involves delving into their feelings, motivations, and patterns. They report mocking therapy and self-help because doing the work was too painful. It was easier to dismiss any type of self-reflection as silly or useless.

The reality, however, is that sobriety comes only with painful self-realization. Addiction is fundamentally a means to escape inner turmoil. The core of therapy and Twelve Step work is *developing a functional relationship with yourself.*

For that to happen, you must find ways to reflect on your recovery work. Readings, meditations, journaling, working the Twelve Steps—whatever path you choose, you must build personal reflection into your life. Further, it is important to allow for regular periods of downtime to do the reflecting. Rest. No activity. Just being with yourself. These "windows of time" are incredibly important to your ability to sort yourself out. Rest and reflection are key to an examined life.

Write about the changes you are making or need to make in your life to find time for quiet reflection.

_____

_____

_____

_____

_____

8. Relationships

Many people have incomplete relationships, at best. People with addictions may struggle with isolation. They handle things on their own, so no one knows just how much they struggle. Most gamers are social online; few are social offline. And they all hide parts of their lives. No one sees the whole picture.

Sadly, there is no way out of shame for the person who lets no one in. Along with accountability, one has to experience the acceptance and help of others to heal. It is the experience of other people's acceptance of you that makes self-acceptance work. One way to make sure recovery is successful is to stay connected with people who know your whole story.

There is a critical other piece to this. Relationships that are face-to-face are the ones that will ultimately restore you. Remember Limbic Resonance? It is those offline, face-to-face relationships that provide you with the experience of limbic resonance that you need to function well. You need to be able to hug your friends, cry on their shoulders, laugh and be frustrated with them. You need to be able to call them to help out in an emergency, to cook together, play Frisbee golf, ride share, hike in the mountains. This is what nourishes you and ends your loneliness. List the people whom you can see in-person who know your whole story.

_____

_____

_____

_____

_____

Now list the people you would like to eventually know your whole story:

_____

_____

_____

_____

_____

9. Affect

Therapists use the word *affect* to describe our emotional lives. Just as we need intellectual skills such as problem-solving, we need emotional skills such as handling anxiety and expressing our feelings.

People struggling with addictive behavior often have "disordered affect," which means they do not handle their emotions well. People who are new to recovery often tell us that they struggle to have and experience feelings. In many ways, in the past they were punished for having feelings. In some families it simply was not acceptable to have an emotional life. Or it may have just been the family norm not to express feelings. To survive in either case, their feeling life was shut down.

There are additional reasons for disordered affect. For example, some people who are smart learn to rely only on their ability to think and neglect the development of their feelings and intuitions. Other people overreact. Simple things escalate into intense emotional drama. Those caught in addiction are particularly prone to using rage to manipulate and intimidate. This rage becomes a self-indulgent extension of "I deserve it" and "I want what I want when I want it!" Volatile and intense relationships become a venue for emotional roller-coaster scripts of disappointment and excitement. The turmoil obscures the anxiety and the emotions underlying the dramatic scenes.

Perhaps the biggest reason for disordered affect is that when life was painful, it was simply easier to numb than to feel. Numbing out is one of the benefits of addiction. It keeps feelings at bay. Whether due to high drama or numbness, the result is the same: core feelings remain unacknowledged.

Recovering people often have to start by labeling the most basic feelings of joy, pain, sadness, anger, and fear. That way, they start to gain clarity about what they are feeling. They learn basic strategies to handle anxiety, such as learning to stay in the here and now rather than stirring themselves up by obsessing about the past or the future. The principles of "letting go" summarized in the Serenity Prayer become a life stance for dealing with anxiety and control.

God grant me

SERENITY

to accept things

I cannot change

COURAGE

to change the

things I can and

WISDOM

to know the difference

People with gaming disorder, in our experience, are typically depressed and anxious. List below some of the thoughts you have that are connected to your depression and anxiety, if you recognize those emotions.

_____

_____

_____

_____

_____

_____

Recovery Essentials

By working on these issues, people notice that the very groundwork of their life changes. They may find that the Internet, screen time, or gaming is not the only issue. The real problem may be the underlying dynamics that provide the addictive system with its power. Also remember that if gaming (for example) had not become the focus of the addiction cycle, it's very possible that something else would have taken its place. The core problem is usually a collage of addictions and deprivations.

To be successful in recovery, there are some essential things to do.

- Do only what is important.
- Reward yourself for good work.
- Affirm yourself.
- Be accountable.
- Take care of yourself.
- Know what matters.
- Learn from mistakes.
- Rest and reflect.
- Connect to those who know your story.
- Allow pain, joy, fear, and anger.
- Stay present.
- Have boundaries with self and others.
- Be vulnerable.

Establishing Balance

Being in recovery means that you have succeeded in maintaining the boundaries you set for yourself around your behavioral addiction for at least three months. We say three months because that is a long enough period for you to have gotten started in living without addictive distractions. Your brain will have gone through the most intensive phase of withdrawal, and new habits of self-care will have started to take root. Any person can abstain from addictive behavior for some period of time without doing the deep work that leads to deep change. But once you've put in at least three months of strong recovery work and managed to maintain your digital media use plan, you've entered the vaulted state of "being in recovery."

Your recovery statement will help you determine what you are making a commitment to do and not to do.

Your Recovery Statement

Your recovery statement is not all about what you can't do. Besides listing activities to avoid, it includes activities to explore. It includes the following three areas:

1. Your Abstinence List (Inner Circle)

This list will include the behaviors that are part of your addiction. For example, if you recognize that Internet use for purposes other than work or school (e.g., gaming, gambling, porn, social media, blogging) is a problem for you, your list will reflect that fact.

2. Your Boundaries List (Middle Circle)

Here you list the situations that could *lead* to a behavior on your abstinence list. For example, going online for any purpose without an accountability buddy checking what you are doing could be harmful to you. So could wandering over to the electronics department of a store to check out computers and the latest game titles. As could using a smartphone rather than a dumbphone.

Engaging in behaviors on your boundaries list creates a hazard to your recovery. It is best to make these items as specific and concrete as possible.

3. Your Balanced Digital Media Plan (Outer Circle/Recovery Behaviors)

This list describes what you are working toward with digital media use, as well as the healthy things that you are putting into your life that will replace unhealthy digital media use and will help to maintain a sustainable lifestyle.

As with the abstinence and the boundaries lists, your writing needs to be very specific.

Completing Your Recovery Statement

These three lists will become your recovery statement. Your therapist, your group, and your sponsor will review and discuss it with you. It becomes an agreed-upon contract about how you will conduct your life. Your recovery statement can change with time. For example, you may discover new behaviors that you need to add to the abstinence list, and you may be able to remove boundaries that are no longer necessary as you become healthier. Over the years, your sobriety statement will become a well-worn document that serves you well.

A) Abstinence List (Inner Circle)

Directions: In recovery, abstinence means avoiding behaviors that you are powerless over and that lead to unmanageability in your life. Doing one of these behaviors again and then talking about it right away with your therapist and recovery community means you've had a slip or lapse; continuing it over a period of time and hiding it means you've had a relapse.

Identify and then list the behaviors that you need to abstain from in your recovery. Be specific and concrete—for example: *No use of the Internet on a computer that does not have accountability software installed and an accountability partner checking the reports.* If you need more room to write, continue on additional paper or in your journal. Also include today's date on this worksheet.

Remember that you may amend, add to, or delete from your abstinence list as circumstances and recovery warrant. Before making a change, however, consult with your group, sponsor, or therapist.

Your Abstinence _____ **As of (date):** _____

1. _____

2. _____

3. _____

4. _____

5. _____

6. _____

7. _____

8. _____

B) Boundaries List (Middle Circle)

Directions: Boundaries are self-imposed limits that promote health and safety. They may involve situations, circumstances, people, and behaviors that you avoid because they are dangerous, because they jeopardize your abstinence, or because they do not add to your recovery or your spirituality. For example: *No watching Youtube for anything but music.* Boundaries are guides to help you toward health. Crossing over a boundary does not signify a relapse. It does, however, signify a need to refocus on priorities.

Below, list boundaries that will help your recovery. Again, be as specific as possible.

Your Boundaries _____ **As of (date):** _____

1. _____

2. _____

3. _____

4. _____

5. _____

6. _____

7. _____

8. _____

C) Plan for Life Balance (Recovery Behaviors)

Directions: Start by listing five goals you have that you believe will help you live a life that is balanced and healthy. If this is difficult for you—and it is for most people—consult with your sponsor, group members, or therapist. Remember, you are looking for areas you wish to improve. These are uncharted waters for many people in early recovery. After writing down your goals, list specific action steps you can take and resources you can use to achieve them.

Example:

Goal: *I would like to check FB once a day for no more than half an hour and use it only to connect with friends and family.*

Action Steps: *I will find an accountability partner (preferably my sponsor), who will help me install protective software on my computer and will agree to check my daily computer usage.*

Resources: *Get help from my sponsor. Ask my recovery friends to bookend my social media sessions.*

1. **Goal:** _____

_____

Action Steps: _____

_____

Resources: _____

_____

2. **Goal:** _____

_____

Action Steps: _____

_____

Resources: _____

_____

3. **Goal:** _____

_____

Action Steps: _____

_____

Resources: _____

_____

4. **Goal:** _____

_____

Action Steps: _____

_____

Resources: _____

_____

5. **Goal:** _____

_____

Action Steps: _____

_____

Resources: _____

_____

Through your recovery work, you will be developing yourself in many ways. Creating your recovery plan will be a crucial step in understanding what healthy boundaries mean for you. These boundaries will be based on your understanding of what you need as you move away from addictive patterns and learn recovery patterns. As time goes by and recovery progresses, you will become clear about your values, you will hold yourself accountable, and you will ask others to hold you accountable, as well. Your self-esteem will grow as your recovery self grows stronger. We hope you can relish the journey, difficult as it can be.

In the next chapter, we will focus on ways to prevent relapse. Once you understand there are things you can do to prevent relapse, you'll be able to recognize the danger signs and not be taken by surprise when they crop up.

Chapter 9

Preventing Relapse –
A return to addictive behaviors

It is not uncommon for people in recovery to have one or more slips or relapses, but it also is not inevitable. If you have one, learn from it. Do you need to tighten up your inner circle behaviors? Is there something new to add to your middle circle? Were you not maintaining your healthy recovery behaviors? As long as you learn from your slip or relapse and get back on the recovery track, it's not a disaster. But it's certainly preferable to avoid slips and relapses altogether. Sometimes the consequences from a slip/relapse can be dire (e.g., parents may refuse to support you any further), so it's worth doing all that you can to prevent it from happening. The work that follows will ask you to think through the steps and thinking that occur that lead you down the wrong path.

Imagine a boulder on top of a hill. The boulder serves as an important stabilizer for all that is around it. You have been given the job of keeping that boulder in place. If it rolls down the hill, it will cause all kinds of damage.

At the bottom of the hill is a large lake. If the boulder hits the water, it will be much more difficult to retrieve; and if the boulder does fall in the lake, it is your job to return it to the top of the hill.

As this big rock sits at rest on top of the hill, it takes little or no effort on your part to keep things in balance. But let us say that the land becomes unstable and the boulder starts to roll down a slippery slope toward the bottom of the hill. Where is the best place for you to intervene?

There are several possible answers to that question. When the boulder is still near the top of the hill, it might take only 20 percent of your strength to stop its momentum. By the time it is halfway down the hill, it might take 100 percent of your ability to stop it. By the time it reaches the bottom of the hill, the boulder might roll with so much speed and power that you cannot stop it. The following figure illustrates the principle of the boulder gaining momentum.

Relapse Prevention: Loss of Control

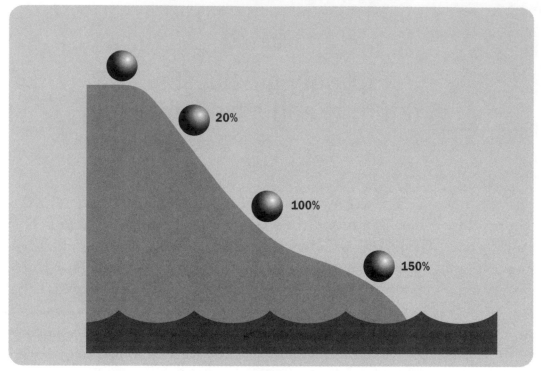

Figure 8.1

Obviously, it is best to keep the boulder stable at the top of the hill. But if you have to stop it from rolling, it is far better to do this when the boulder is still near the hilltop. By the time the boulder reaches the bottom, your last-ditch efforts might not be enough to save it.

So it is with recovery; it is better to keep stable in recovery or intervene early in the face of potential relapse. The most important strategy for this is to create a recovery zone. The recovery zone is a lifestyle with certain parameters. If you stay inside them, you will be safe. The trick is creating those parameters.

Claiming Your Recovery Zone: The Personal Chaos Index (PCI)

Most of us have had the experience of being really "on." Everything clicks together. Problems are simply problems. Facing complicated challenges is manageable, and you feel great. There is an optimum zone of psychological and physical health for each of us. An essential task in life is to figure out how to stay in that zone. Recovery, in many ways, is the reclaiming of that zone as you emerge from addictive illness.

Recovery is much like training for athletes. Olympic competitors and professional athletes know that to succeed, they will experience great stress. Therefore, they train and prepare for it. They work every day to face the stressful event, be it a game or tournament. Similarly, recovering people prepare every day so that a stressor will not be overwhelming. They plan, they practice, they develop skills and strategies. They build their stamina and reserves so they can perform consistently. Sponsors and therapists provide coaching so that when the challenge comes, the addict is prepared.

Some years ago, Dr. Patrick Carnes and his team developed a self-assessment process called the Personal Craziness Index, which we now refer to as The Personal Chaos Index (PCI). Over the years, it has helped many people establish the basic parameters of their recovery zone. It starts with the basic practices that help us be "on." Put another way, it keeps the boulder in place.

The PCI is based on two assumptions. First, disruption manifests itself as lapses in routine and simple behaviors that support self-maintenance. Second, signs of life disruption will occur in several different areas of life. Thus, we can be caught up in issues of cosmic importance and fail to notice that our checking account is overdrawn. If our checking account is overdrawn, then we are probably out of socks, as well, because we neglected to do our laundry. And on and on it can go.

Those with addictions are particularly susceptible to this loss of balance due to neglecting the basics of daily life. "Keep it simple," "One day at a time," and other slogans are not shopworn clichés, but guidelines born from the experience of many in recovery.

The PCI serves as a daily reminder of what we need to do. Without a process for such reminders, "cunning and baffling" self-destructive behavior returns. When people actually observe and work their PCI process, they dramatically reduce the potential for relapse. To do this well takes time—and you may wish to refine the process as you go. The daily self-assessment of your PCI keeps you mindful of your recovery zone.

Creating Your Personal Chaos Index

Directions: The process of creating your own PCI is designed to be as value-free as possible. Each person uses the index by setting his or her own criteria. In other words, discover the behavioral signs that in your experience indicate that you are feeling out of control, burnt out, or stressed. These are warnings that the boulder is ready to roll. Thus, it is by your own standards that you prepare yourself.

Following are twelve dimensions of your life in which you will identify danger signs that can indicate your behavior is unsustainable. Write your answers to each of the questions in the space provided.

The twelve dimensions are:

- Physical Health
- Transportation
- Environment
- Work
- Interests
- Social Life

- Family and Significant Others
- Finances
- Spiritual Life and Personal Reflection
- Other Compulsive or Symptomatic Behaviors
- Twelve Step Practice and Therapeutic Self-Care
- Healthy Relationships

For purposes of this book, we are adding a thirteenth dimension, sexuality, so you can keep an eye on that aspect of your life as well.

1. Physical Health. The ultimate insanity is not to take care of our body. When our physical health deteriorates, we have nothing. Yet we seem to have little time for physical conditioning. Examples of "craziness" in this area of life include being over a certain weight, missing regular exercise for two days or more, smoking more cigarettes than usual, and feeling exhausted from lack of sleep.

How do you know that you are not taking care of your body? (List at least three examples.)

1. _____

2. _____

3. _____

4. _____

5. _____

2. Transportation. How people get from place to place is often a statement about lifestyle. Take, for example, a car owner who seldom comes to a full stop, routinely exceeds the speed limit, runs out of gas, forgets to check the oil, puts off needed repairs, neglects to clean the backseat, and averages three speeding tickets and ten parking tickets per year. Another example is the bus rider who routinely misses the bus, forgets to carry change, or frequently leaves a briefcase or purse on the bus.

What are the transportation behaviors that indicate your life is getting out of control? (List at least three examples.)

1. _____

2. _____

3. _____

4. _____

5. _____

3. Environment. Not to have time to do your personal chores is a comment on the order of your life. Consider the home in which the plants usually go unwatered, fish are unfed, grocery supplies are depleted, laundry is not done or put away, cleaning is neglected, and dishes go unwashed.

What are ways in which you neglect your home or living space?
(List at least three examples.)

1. _____

2. _____

3. _____

4. _____

5. _____

4. Work/school. Chaos at work or school is risky for recovery. Signs of chaotic behavior are failing to return phone calls within twenty-four hours, not studying for an exam, showing up late for appointments, not showing up for classes, falling behind in work, having an unmanageable in-basket or class load, and putting "too many irons in the fire."

When your life is unmanageable at work, what are your behaviors? (List at least three examples.)

1. _____

2. _____

3. _____

4. _____

5. _____

5. Interests. What are some positive interests, besides work, that give you perspective on the world? Music, reading, photography, fishing, or gardening are examples.

What are you doing when you are not overextended? (List at least three examples.)

1. _____

2. _____

3. _____

4. _____

5. _____

6. Social Life. Think of friends in your social network (beyond a significant other and family members) who provide significant support for you.

What are signs that you've become isolated, alienated, or disconnected from this network? (List at least three examples.)

1. _____

2. _____

3. _____

4. _____

5. _____

7. **Family and Significant Others.** Examples of craziness in this area of life are staying silent, becoming overtly hostile, or engaging in passive-aggressive behaviors.

What behaviors indicate that you are disconnected from those closest to you? (List at least three examples.)

1. _____

2. _____

3. _____

4. _____

5. _____

8. **Finances.** We handle our financial resources much like our personal resources. Signs of financial overextension include an unbalanced checking account, overdue bills, a lack of ready cash, and spending more than you earn. These may have parallels in various forms of emotional overextension.

What signs indicate that you are financially overextended? (List at least three examples.)

1. _____

2. _____

3. _____

4. _____

5. _____

9. Spiritual Life and Personal Reflection. Spirituality can be diverse and include such activities as meditation, yoga, and prayer. Personal reflection includes keeping a personal journal, completing daily readings, and pursuing therapy.

What sources of routine personal reflection do you neglect when you are overextended? (List at least three examples.)

1. _____

2. _____

3. _____

4. _____

5. _____

10. Other Compulsive or Symptomatic Behaviors. Compulsive behaviors that have negative consequences indicate something about your general wellbeing and state of overall recovery. When you watch inordinate amounts of TV, overeat, bite your nails, or develop another compulsive behavior that erodes your self-esteem, these can be signs of burnout or possible unhealthy coping mechanisms. Symptomatic behaviors such as forgetfulness, slips of the tongue, or jealousy are further evidence of overextension.

What negative compulsive or symptomatic behaviors are present when you feel "on the edge"? (List at least three examples.)

1. _____

2. _____

3. _____

4. _____

5. _____

11. Twelve Step Practice and Therapeutic Self-Care. Living a Twelve Step way of life involves many practices. Group attendance, Step work, sponsorship, service, and Twelve Step phone calls to support group members become the foundation of a good recovery. For some partners attending therapy, their method of self-care may be being involved in a facilitated support group. *Which recovery activities do you neglect first?* (List at least three examples.)

1. _____

2. _____

3. _____

4. _____

5. _____

12. Healthy Relationships. Engaging in exploitative, abusive, or otherwise unhealthy relationships is a sign that you are not well grounded in your recovery.

What are signs that a relationship of yours is unhealthy or becoming unhealthy? Are you lying to the other person in the relationship or leaving out important pieces of the truth? Are you afraid to say what's on your mind? Are your boundaries still firm, or are you doing things someone else wants you to do even when it's not right for you? (List at least three examples.)

1. _____

2. _____

3. _____

4. _____

5. _____

Relapse Scenario Worksheets

It is critical to have the total picture of your addictive cycle so you can define what it means for you to be in recovery. To simply say "I will not play any more video games" is not enough. You will also need to carefully map out the most likely ways you will act out and then eliminate the roads that lead there. This process is called *relapse prevention planning*. It means identifying the most likely scenarios of relapse and then detailing what you will do when faced with these or similar scenarios.

The following three worksheets are designed to help you do this work.

- Under *probable preconditions present*, list factors that may change your general mood, whether positive or negative, such as boredom, loneliness, anxiety, exhaustion, anger, feeling celebratory, or feeling overwhelmed.

- Under *personal recovery challenges present*, include whatever issues you have identified as potential problems within yourself that could contribute to a relapse scenario. List such things as entitlement, perfectionism, compulsive busyness, social avoidance, or ignoring common sense. (For more ideas, review the section about recovery challenges in Chapter 8.)

Challenges of Recovery		
• Underachieving despair • Self-defeating shame • Not being accountable • Profound self-neglect • No remorse • No common sense • Avoidance/procrastination • Isolation • Shutdown feelings/ numbness	• Distorted achievement • Compromised self-image • Lack of accountability • Problematic self-care • Impaired conscience • Faulty realism • Limited self-awareness • Incomplete relationships • Disordered affect	• Overachieving depletion and chaos • Self-absorbed obsession • Secret life • Grandiose entitlement • Guilt-driven behavior • Common sense ignored • Compulsive busyness • Hidden parts of self • Indulgent rage, drama, intensity

- Fill in the "staircase" section of the worksheet. On top of each step (next to a number), list a behavior or event that would lead you to compulsive behavior. Underneath each step, briefly summarize the related self-talk—what you would say to yourself to justify taking the step. See if you can lay out the steps in the order they are most likely to happen.

- What is the worst that could happen if you relapse? List these under *worst possible consequences*.

- Under *probable consequences*, describe what is *most likely* to happen if you relapse.
- When you have completed each scenario, title it at the top of the worksheet. For example, Path to Gaming, or Path to Internet Surfing.

When you have completed the Relapse Scenario Worksheets, share them with your therapist, group, and sponsor. To help get you started, please review the following Relapse Scenario sample worksheet for Ian, 19, who originally was from South Africa. He had spent some of his youth in the US, he and his mother having dual citizenship. He was accepted to a university but struggled and entered treatment after his first semester. Although he did what was asked of him, he always expressed his belief that he "got it," that it would be relatively easy to return to college, abstain from gaming, and do well. We did not think he was ready to return to college and asked him to stay and engage in deeper recovery work and to practice living a sustainable lifestyle in the face of challenges. However, he refused and returned to the city where he planned to start back at college in the fall. His mother rented an apartment for him. He had turned over his computer to her, but, as he had access to money, he bought another computer and soon he was gaming again. Alone and isolated, gaming as heavily as before, he proceeded to regain the 25 pounds he'd lost while in treatment. And when classes started, he failed to show up for them, effectively dropping out after a couple of months.

Fortunately, his parents were willing to send him back for a second round of treatment. This time he examined and understood the thinking that led to his relapse. He more fully participated in the program and developed a tight relapse prevention plan, and to this day, he is thriving. In the following sample relapse prevention exercise are the steps he took toward relapse and the thinking that accompanied each.

Sample Relapse Scenario Worksheet

Scenario 1: Ian's story above

Probable preconditions present

1. Academic demands were high
2. He didn't recognize how difficult it would be to return to college without completing Phase 2 of the treatment program.
3. He was anxious to get back to the world he knew.
4. He did not want to do all the work required to really "get recovery"
5. He moved back to the old city and university.
6. He bought a gaming-capable computer.
7. He did not go to Twelve Step meetings or meet with a sponsor.
8. He watched YouTube videos about gaming.

Personal Recovery Challenges present

1. Grandiose entitlement.
2. Overachieving depletion
3. Not accountable.
4. Isolation.
5. Avoidance/procrastination.
6. Shutdown feelings/numbness.

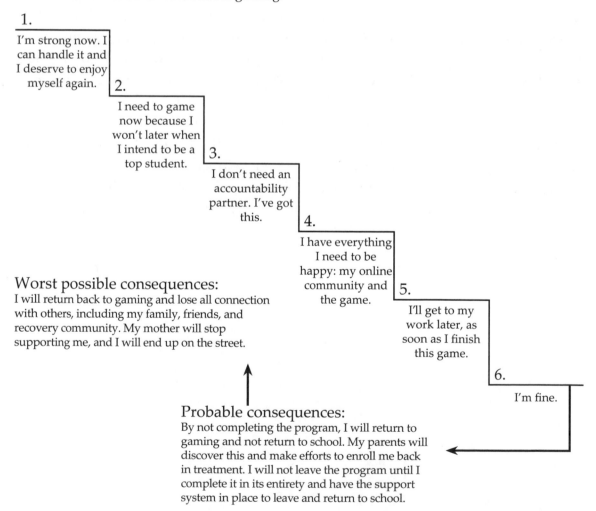

1.
I'm strong now. I can handle it and I deserve to enjoy myself again.

2.
I need to game now because I won't later when I intend to be a top student.

3.
I don't need an accountability partner. I've got this.

4.
I have everything I need to be happy: my online community and the game.

5.
I'll get to my work later, as soon as I finish this game.

6.
I'm fine.

Worst possible consequences:
I will return back to gaming and lose all connection with others, including my family, friends, and recovery community. My mother will stop supporting me, and I will end up on the street.

Probable consequences:
By not completing the program, I will return to gaming and not return to school. My parents will discover this and make efforts to enroll me back in treatment. I will not leave the program until I complete it in its entirety and have the support system in place to leave and return to school.

With this worksheet, you can see how Ian justified and rationalized each step of the way until he was right back in it.

Now, it's your turn to think through as many scenarios as you can where you will be tempted to relapse. These are *triggers*. *Rationalizations* are the thoughts that you will use to convince yourself it is all right to give in to the urges you feel when you are triggered.

Relapse Scenario Worksheet 1

Scenario 1: _____

Probable preconditions present

1. _____

2. _____

3. _____

4. _____

Personal Recovery Challenges present

1. _____

2. _____

3. _____

4. _____

1.
Self-Talk
_____

_____

2.
Self-Talk
_____

_____

3.
Self-Talk
_____

_____

4.
Self-Talk
_____

_____

5.
Self-Talk
_____

_____

6.

Worst possible consequences:

_____

_____

Probable consequences:

_____

_____

Relapse Scenario Worksheet 2

Scenario 2: _____

Probable preconditions present

1. _____

2. _____

3. _____

4. _____

Personal Recovery Challenges present

1. _____

2. _____

3. _____

4. _____

1.
Self-Talk
_____

2.
Self-Talk
_____

3.
Self-Talk
_____

4.
Self-Talk
_____

5.
Self-Talk
_____

6.

Worst possible consequences:

_____

_____

Probable consequences:

_____

_____

Relapse Scenario Worksheet 3

Scenario 3: _____

Probable preconditions present

1. _____

2. _____

3. _____

4. _____

Personal Recovery Challenges present

1. _____

2. _____

3. _____

4. _____

1.
_____
Self-Talk

_____

_____

2.
_____
Self-Talk

_____

_____

3.
_____
Self-Talk

_____

_____

4.
_____
Self-Talk

_____

5.
_____
Self-Talk

_____

_____

6.
_____

Worst possible consequences:

_____

_____

Probable consequences:

_____

_____

Fire Drill Planning

Directions: A fire drill is an exercise in planning and practicing what to do in an emergency. It includes a routine set of steps put into action immediately, should trouble be near. This is an automatic protection plan that depends on three elements:

- A clear alarm (a clear sign of trouble).
- Concrete steps to be taken.
- A routine way to practice the concrete steps.

To begin, review the Relapse Scenario Worksheets you completed. Then complete this exercise. First, enter specific signs that there may be a potential relapse. Then describe action steps you will take. Finally, indicate how you can practice those action steps. Remember that the success of your plan depends on how specific you can make it.

When you're done, show this worksheet to your group, sponsor, and therapist. Ask them for feedback on the steps you have listed. Encourage them to be honest and be willing to listen. It could make a huge difference later. This extra effort on your part, along with the scenario worksheets, will help you to create a thorough definition of sobriety.

Symptom or Sign of Trouble	Immediate Action Steps	Practice (Drill) Steps
Example: Watching a YouTube gaming video	*Example: Call my sponsor*	*Example: Call my sponsor regularly*
1.	1.	1.
2.	2.	2.
3.	3.	3.

Symptom or Sign of Trouble	Immediate Action Steps	Practice (Drill) Steps
4.	4.	4.
5.	5.	5.
6.	6.	6.
7.	7.	7.
8.	8.	8.
9.	9.	9.
10.	10.	10.

A Letter from You to Yourself

Directions: Imagine you are your sponsor writing a letter to yourself just at the time you want to engage in addictive behavior. What would you say? By writing the letter and carrying it with you, you have a significant resource to pull out at the last minute. Address this letter from you to yourself. Include answers to the following questions:

1. What are the probable circumstances under which it is being read?
2. What are the consequences if you ignore the letter?
3. What would you really need at the time of a slip?
4. What clear criteria for addictive behavior can you give yourself?
5. What is the hope if you don't act out?
6. What is at stake if you *do* relapse—what is the plea from your recovery self to your addict self that you need to hear at this moment?

Take your letter to your group. Have your sponsor and group members write notes on the letter itself. Then when you read it, you will have their support as well. It may help you keep your sobriety. The following is a sample letter.

Dear Chris,

When you feel the urge, pull out this letter. Chances are, if you are reading it, you are experiencing a pleasurable thrill at the thought of accessing your technology. Please read to the end because if the thought is about relapsing, chances are you are alone. So please keep reading.

Each time is the same. There is the thought—the pleasure. There is the anger, the loneliness, the feelings of entitlement. But remember, every time is the same; you will regret terribly what you now want to do.

*   *You will have to worry about the consequences.*
*   *You will feel depressed or anxious.*
*   *You will despair over your broken commitments.*

- *You will feel pain at the people you used.*
- *You will have to tell lies to cover up—always there are lies.*
- *You will have suicidal feelings.*
- *You will place all your career success in jeopardy.*
- *You will never enjoy it—you are always disappointed.*
- *You become more isolated.*

Right now, your addict is seducing you with promises that won't work. So, figure out what you need:

- *Are you hungry or tired?*
- *Are you angry?*
- *Are you overextended?*
- *Are you needing care?*

Find whatever you need and get it. Do not do the one thing that will make all of the above worse.

You are lovable and worthwhile. You deserve to get your needs met in a way that respects your wonderfulness. Imagine spirituality that is peaceful, graceful, vibrant, and growing—not what you are experiencing now.

Please listen to yourself. You know that the life you want won't happen for you by relapsing. Do not kid yourself. Instead, love yourself enough to let it pass. Let it go. Call someone.

Love,
   Chris

Emergency Self-Care Kit

Directions: Make a psychological emergency self-care kit. It can be a bag, a "medicine pouch," an envelope, or even a box. Place things that provide your life with meaning inside of it. Suggestions include:

- Symbols of recovery, including medallions, tokens, sponsor gifts, and other articles that remind you of significant moments in your recovery.
- Pictures and mementos of loved ones.
- Spiritual items.
- Copies of pages out of this book.
- Letters.
- Favorite affirmations, meditations, or quotes.
- Phone numbers of peers and sponsors.
- Any items that represent personal meaning to you.
- Music that is special to you.

Keep this kit in a place that is easy for you to find. If you feel you are about to relapse or already have slipped, pull out the kit to get support for what you need to do.

Relapse Contract

Directions: Use the following contract as a way to talk to important people (such as your sponsor, therapist, and clergyperson) about what you will do if you do slip. Make a copy of the contract for that person and keep a copy for yourself.

I, _____ (*your name*), do agree (contract) that if I have a slip in my recovery, I will do the following:

- I will make my very best effort to limit what I have done.
- I will call you and let you know what my situation is.
- I will do the following (*fill in whatever you and your support person think should be the first steps*):

_____

_____

_____

My recovery date is: _____

Agreed to on this date: _____

Signed, _____

Being successful in long-term recovery is all about building your support system. We'll learn more about that in the following chapter.

Chapter 10

What Makes for Long-Term Success?
Deepening Recovery for Profound Life Change

Jerry is a young man who came into recovery for his gaming addiction. He had, as is typical, failed out of his first year of college. His parents were worried that he might be suicidal because they could see that he was deeply depressed and unstable. They did an intervention, and through that, he agreed to enroll in treatment. He did well in the intensive phase (a stress-free retreat), but in the transition program that followed, he became obsessed with a young woman who was not interested in him romantically. Jerry did not have good tools for handling this kind of emotional stress. He had not gotten a sponsor, despite our recommendation to do so, and was not going regularly to any Twelve Step meetings.

He did not confide in anyone how he was feeling or that he was slipping into addictive thinking, feeling an intense desire to escape his hurt and angry feelings. In secret, he started taking drugs, something he had never done before. One night, high and feeling scared of how his body felt, he called a friend. This friend, another man in recovery from Internet gaming addiction, took him to the hospital where he was kept under close watch until the doctors said he was out of danger. His parents were alerted and it was agreed that he needed to go into treatment for what was now a drug problem.

When Jerry was in that treatment facility, he finally came to understand the importance of Twelve Step work, showing up honestly, having a sponsor, and staying away from dating while in early recovery. Upon his return, he found a nine-month educational program that steeped him in learning about the natural world, indigenous spiritual practices, and how to have fun. Finally, engaged with something in the real world that interested him passionately, he thrived socially, physically, and spiritually. His commitment to recovery has remained strong. He is now working full time, has a lovely girlfriend, and has discovered the career path he wants to pursue.

Jerry's case illustrates both how recovery can fail when the right steps are not taken, and how it can succeed when they are.

Patrick Carnes and his researchers wanted to learn more about the people who had gotten better, to see what actions and thoughts contributed to their success.

What they discovered was much more revealing than they had ever anticipated. They found many measures of quality of life and health. They found that people in recovery made dramatic changes for the better in their lives. They also found that the people who had the greatest success took the same steps in a relatively predictable fashion. Recovery was but one of their life changes. They all had made a deeper commitment to making their lives better.

An overall pattern emerged. Here is the general profile of those who succeeded in recovery:

- **They had a primary therapist.** Whether they went to residential programs, intensive workshops, or took part in specialized therapy with others, each was involved with a therapist with whom they stayed over a three- to five-year period. Working through a relationship with a therapist appears to be essential to recovery. Even more important, they each allowed themselves to have an examined life in which one person (the therapist) knew them extraordinarily well and had skills to help them through the challenges they encountered as they progressed in their recovery.

- **They were in a therapy group.** Whether some of these hours were in a residential or outpatient setting seemed to make little difference. Those who did well spent time in a group setting with a therapist (who might or might not be their primary therapist). The optimum amount of time in such a group was approximately 175 hours over a period of eighteen months to two years.

- **They regularly went to Twelve Step meetings.** Those who succeeded in recovery became deeply involved in the program, including participation in service, sponsorship, and Step work. Working through all the Steps makes a critical difference; those who did not continue Step work either struggled in their recovery or lost it altogether.

- **If other addictions were present, they were addressed as well.** People went to other Twelve Step meetings as appropriate for them. They came to understand how their addictions interacted (negatively!) with one another and how they all related to the deeper problems in their lives.

- **They worked to clarify and resolve their family-of-origin and childhood issues.** They used the Steps and therapy to understand the deeper character issues they faced, and they did everything they could do to find serenity with them.

- **Their families were involved early in therapy.** Clearly, early family involvement and support plays a significant role in recovery. We found a clear difference between people who were involved on their own in treatment and those whose partners and family members committed to therapy and recovery for themselves. Often, the addict's recovery was the impetus for recovery and healing in other family members, though in some cases years passed before this happened.

- **They developed a spiritual life.** What their spiritual life consisted of was as important as practicing it on a regular, even daily, basis. Those whose spiritual life flourished were also usually active participants in a spiritual community.

- **They actively worked to maintain regular exercise and good nutrition.** Those whose recovery blossomed exercised regularly, if not daily, and were also conscientious about making good food choices as part of their self-care.

Directions: What are you willing to do to create a healthy, balanced life in recovery? What do you envision this life will look like tomorrow? What do you think it will look like in ten years? As you think about this, think about the 24 hours in an average day. If you made a pie chart, what would it look like?

 We've given you four pie charts. Take the time to fill in one for an ideal, sustainable lifestyle for a weekday in your current life, and another for a weekend day in your current life. The other two are for how you would like your sober life to look in ten years—one for a weekday and one for the weekend.

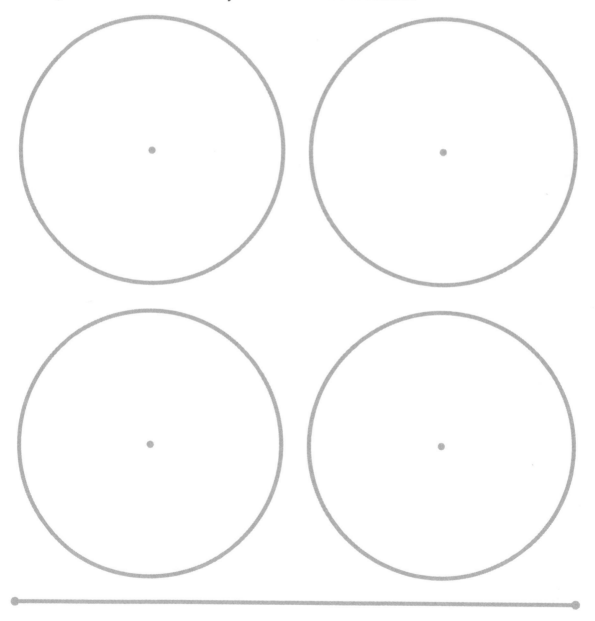

Celebrate

Now we ask you to think about your life. You've done the exercises in this book. You've read about what research tells us are the ingredients for long-term success in recovery. Allow yourself to dream about what a deeply satisfying life looks and feels like for you. Then go out and have some fun creating your new life.

Appendix A
The Twelve Steps of Alcoholics Anonymous

1. We admitted we were powerless over alcohol—that our lives had become unmanageable.

2. Came to believe that a Power greater than ourselves could restore us to sanity.

3. Made a decision to turn our will and our lives over to the care of God as *we understood Him.*

4. Made a searching and fearless moral inventory of ourselves.

5. Admitted to God, to ourselves, and to another human being the exact nature of our wrongs.

6. Were entirely ready to have God remove all these defects of character.

7. Humbly asked Him to remove our shortcomings.

8. Made a list of all persons we had harmed, and became willing to make amends to them all.

9. Made direct amends to such people wherever possible, except when to do so would injure them or others.

10. Continued to take personal inventory and when we were wrong promptly admitted it.

11. Sought through prayer and meditation to improve our conscious contact with God as *we understood Him*, praying only for knowledge of His will for us and the power to carry that out.

12. Having had a spiritual awakening as the result of these steps, we tried to carry this message to alcoholics, and to practice these principles in all our affairs.

The Twelve Steps of AA are from *Alcoholics Anonymous*, 4th ed., published by AA World Services, Inc., New York, NY, 59–60.

Appendix B
The Twelve Steps for Sex Addicts

The Twelve Steps of Alcoholics Anonymous Adapted for Sexual Addicts

1. We admitted we were powerless over our sexual addiction—that our lives had become unmanageable.
2. Came to believe a Power greater than ourselves could restore us to sanity.
3. Made a decision to turn our will and our lives over to the care of God, as *we understood Him.*
4. Made a searching and fearless moral inventory of ourselves.
5. Admitted to God, to ourselves, and to another human being the exact nature of our wrongs.
6. Were entirely ready to have God remove all these defects of character.
7. Humbly asked Him to remove our shortcomings.
8. Made a list of all persons we had harmed, and became willing to make amends to them all.
9. Made direct amends to such people wherever possible, except when to do so would injure them or others.
10. Continued to take personal inventory and when we were wrong promptly admitted it.
11. Sought through prayer and meditation to improve our conscious contact with God as *we understood Him,* praying only for knowledge of His will for us and the power to carry that out.
12. Having had a spiritual awakening as the result of these steps, we tried to carry this message to others and to practice these principles in all our affairs.

Adapted from the Twelve Steps of Alcoholics Anonymous. Reprinted with permission of AA World Services, Inc., New York, NY.

Appendix C

Twelve Steps and Principles for Internet & Technology Addiction Recovery

1. **Honesty.** Admit that you, or yourself, are powerless to overcome your addictions and that your life has become unmanageable.

2. **Hope.** Come to believe that the power greater than ourselves can restore you to health.

3. **Trust.** Decide to turn your will and your life over to the care of your higher power as you understand it.

4. **Truth.** Make a searching and fearless written moral inventory of yourself.

5. **Integrity.** Admit to yourself, to your higher power, and another human being the exact nature of your wrongs.

6. **Change of heart.** Become entirely ready to have your higher power remove all your character defects.

7. **Humility.** Humbly ask your higher power to remove your shortcomings.

8. **Brotherly love.** Make a written list of all persons you have harmed and become willing to make restitution to them.

9. **Restitution and reconciliation.** Wherever possible, make direct restitution to all persons you have harmed, except when to do so would injure them or others.

10. **Accountability.** Continue to take personal inventory, and when you are wrong promptly admit it.

11. **Spirituality.** Seek through prayer and meditation to improve your conscious contact with a Power greater than ourselves, asking for guidance and the will to carry through on what you know you need to do.

12. **Service.** Having had a spiritual awakening as a result of these steps, share this message with others who excessively use technology, and practice these principles in all you do.

Appendix D

Twelve Steps and Principles for Internet & Technology Addiction Recovery (For Agnostics and Atheists)

1. **Honesty and acceptance.** Admit that you, by yourself, are powerless to overcome your addictions and that your life has become unmanageable.
2. **Hope.** Come to believe that a power greater than ourselves can restore you to health.
3. **Trust.** Decide to turn your will and your life over to a trusted other and be willing to ask for help.
4. **Truth.** Make a searching and fearless written moral inventory of yourself.
5. **Integrity.** Admit to yourself and another human being the exact nature of your wrongs.
6. **Change of heart.** Become entirely ready to work on and remove all your character defects.
7. **Humility.** Be willing to address and change your shortcomings.
8. **Brotherly love.** Make a written list of all persons you have harmed and become willing to make restitution to them.
9. **Restitution and reconciliation.** Wherever possible, make direct restitution to all persons you have harmed, except when to do so would injure them or others.
10. **Accountability.** Continue to take personal inventory, and when you are wrong promptly admit it.
11. **Spirituality.** Seek through prayer and meditation to improve your conscious contact with a Power greater than ourselves, asking for guidance and the will to carry through on what you know you need to do.
12. **Service.** Having had a spiritual awakening as a result of these steps, share this message with others who excessively use technology, and practice these principles in all you do.